苏州博物馆
SUZHOU MUSEUM

Chief Editors: Zhang Xin

Deputy Chief Editors: Lu Man, Qian Gonglin, Zhang Zhaogen, Mao Yan, Yang Wentao

Publishing consultant: Li Peiyi

Executive Editor: Xu Hua

Chinese contributors: Wei Baoxin, Ma Yan

English Editors: Antony White, Cui Jing

English translation: Haiyao Zheng

English Proofreaders: Lin Wen, Jin Di

Designer: Wang Chao

All text and images: Suzhou Museum

This edition ©2007 London Editions (HK) Ltd.

Except images 2, 3, 4, 5, 6, 7, 8, 9: © Fotoe

ISBN: 978-7-80017-881-8/J · 772

First published in 2007 by

Great Wall Publishers

Suzhou Museum

In collaboration with

London Editions, Hong Kong

Antony White

9, Orme Court

London W2 4RL

- -

图书在版编目（ＣＩＰ）数据

苏州博物馆：英文、张欣主编. —北京：长城出版社，
2007. 8
　ISBN　978-7-80017-881-8

　I. 苏⋯　II. 张⋯　III. 博物馆－简介－苏州市－画册
IV. G269. 275. 33-64

中国版本图书馆CIP数据核字（2007）第119889号
- -

Contents

Foreword

The Suzhou Museum, founded in 1960 and dedicated to the local history and culture of Suzhou, was originally housed in the Palace of Zhong Wangfu – the most complete memorial to the history of the Taiping Heavenly Kingdom, whose revolutionary army captured the city in 1860.

The new Suzhou Museum, built by the internationally famous I. M. Pei, was opened to the public in October 2006. Located at the crossroads of Dongbei Street and Qimen Road, the museum comprises Pei's new building of about 10,700 square metres and the original Zhong Wang Fu building, now fully restored, of 26,500 square metres. As a building it adjoins the Humble Administrator's Garden, the Lion Forest Garden and other famous scenic parks, all listed as UNESCO World Heritage sites. Together they create a rich and colourful cultural ensemble.

Over the years the Suzhou Museum has expanded its collections, arranged more than two hundred exhibitions, and undertaken much academic and archaeological research – and attracted more than six million visitors. As the sole local academy at Suzhou authorised by the State Administration of Cultural Heritage for archaeological investigation and excavation, the staff of the Suzhou Museum has to date excavated hundreds of ancient sites and ancient tombs, and compiled and published twenty academic books and magazines. The academic research team has published more than two hundred articles in domestic and foreign academic magazines.

The Suzhou Museum owns more than 30,000 objects amongst which about 250 pieces are Grade One State Cultural Relics, 1,100 are pieces of Grade Two status and 13,000 pieces of Grade Three. The highlights include paintings and calligraphy, ceramics and Ming and Qing Dynasty art.

The programme of temporary exhibitions, and the 3,600 square metre exhibition area, will be crucial to the future establishment of the Suzhou museum as a cultural centre.

The permanent displays are based on the displays of specifically Suzhou art: the National Treasures from the Wu Pagodas, Wu arts and crafts and Wu paintings and calligraphy. In addition the Zhong Wang Fu, apart from being an historic building in itself, houses the splendid collection donated by Mr Zhang Zongxian from Hong Kong. It also houses a period exhibition of the Taiping Heavenly Kingdom.

Suzhou is a city with 2,500 years of history. The Suzhou Museum is the epitome of that history and of the very special garden and water culture for which Suzhou is famous. It is a fitting tribute to the unique local character of one of China's most beautiful cities.

Not only is Suzhou is one of the great historic cities of China – it is also a key site in the agriculturally and culturally fertile Yangtze Delta. Famed worldwide since the days of Marco Polo as 'the Venice of the East', Suzhou is regarded by the Chinese as the cradle of Wu culture, one of the high points of their civilization; twinned with nearby Hangzhou the two cities are admired as 'heaven on earth'.

Situated in modern day Jiangsu province on the lower reaches of the Yangtze and on the shores of Lake Taihu, it is a city of canals and gardens and of beautiful scenery; and a capital of the land of tea, rice, fish and silk.

The earliest remains of a history that streches back 10,000 years can be found on Sanshan Island. 5,000 years later it was a centre of Liangzhu Neolithic culture.

Some 2,500 years later in 514 BC, during the Spring and Autumn Period, King Helu of Wu founded the great city of Helu – later to be re-named Suzhou in 514 AD during the Sui Dynasty. King Helu died in 496 BC and was buried on Tiger Hill (Huqiu).

The city grew in wealth and fame, its economic prosperity hugely boosted by the completion of the Grand Canal in the early 600s which gave it a strategic presence on the entire nation's trade routes.

In 1229, during the Song Dynasty, arguably the high point of ancient China's cultural achievement, an engraved map on a stele (stone tablet) showed the astonishingly advanced urban plan for the city, a chessboard pattern of water, land, lakes, streets, stone bridges and pagodas, that define the town to the present day. From the outset the physical appearance of the city of Suzhou set the background for the great southern renaissance of culture and poetry that occurred south of the Yangzte – the home of great statesmen, poets, playwrights, painters and scientists. It was a great centre for the handicrafts, including wooden carvings from Tao Hua Wu, for fine silks, for local Kunqu and Suzhou opera and for Pingtan, a local form of storytelling in sung ballad form.

Contemporary Suzhou blends the taste and culture of its past with its newly created commercial wealth. The new museum built by Pei is a perfect reflection of this achievement.

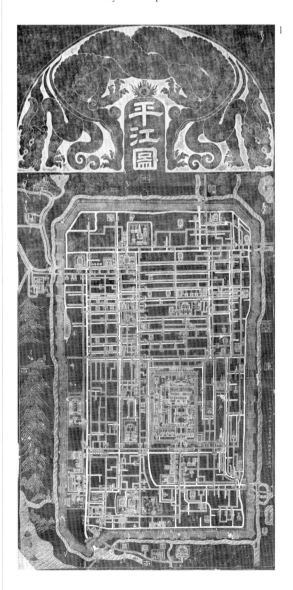

1　Map of Pingjiang, Song Dynasty urban plan

2　Suzhou canal scene (opposite)

3

4

5

6

8

I. M. Pei and the new Suzhou Museum

I. M. Pei is one of the most significant architects of the twentieth century - the leading Chinese architect of world fame. Born in Guangzhou on April 26, 1917, his ancestors were of a noble Suzhou family. As a child he lived in the Pei family house in the Suzhou Lion Forest Garden – a few yards from the new museum. He left China in the mid thirties and studied architecture at MIT and Harvard. He has worked on public buildings in Canada, France, Germany, Australia, Japan, Luxembourg, Qatar, Singapore, Iran, Taiwan, Hong Kong and mainland China. His life work, more than seventy buildings, includes institutes, business centres and skyscrapers. He has won 50 awards including, in 1983, the Pritzker Architecture Prize.

1

In 1999, to reflect the booming growth of Suzhou's economy, and the aspirations of its citizens, the Municipal Government decided to build a new Suzhou Museum. After seven years of site selection, design, demolition, construction and installation, the new Suzhou Museum designed by Pei was opened in the autumn of 2006.

This building reflects the continuity of the architectural style of historical Suzhou and embodies Pei's design philosophy of tradition, innovation and diversity. It blends with its neighbouring gardens and landscapes - each reflecting and enhancing the others' glories.

The new Suzhou Museum faces south. The central section includes the entrance, entrance court, lobby and museum garden. The western section is the major exhibition area; the east area is the minor exhibition area and administrative offices. The central axis of the layout matches that of Zhong Wang Fu. To preserve the historical style of the area, the Suzhou Museum adopts a plan of one underground floor and one ground floor with a

3

cornice height of the backbone of the building of less than six metres. The great lobby and west exhibition area uses in parts a two floor structure with a height of sixteen metres. This ensures that none of the neighbouring buildings is overshadowed. To the south of the front gate there is a pedestrianised street and small square near the river. Both sides of the street are lined with ancient buildings, well preserved and of classical elegance.

The Suzhou Museum uses the traditional elements of white walls and black tiles in a new contemporary context. In terms of structure, the design at the roof configuration overcomes the lack of light in traditional Chinese building by employing a glass and open steel structure to make the indoor full of daylight.

The landscape design in the garden at the new Suzhou Museum derives from the classic Chinese garden, which integrates organically the innovative landscape with the elements of pool, artificial rockery, small bridge, pavilion and bamboo with the traditional Suzhou garden.

Pei has used Chinese style with innovation, and Suzhou style with creativity; and has blended them with the idea of "not too high, not too large and not too abrupt" – a true mixture of the ancient and modern, of Suzhou style brought up to date. It not only creates an iconic public building for the city of Suzhou but represents a new international development in Chinese architecture.

2

1   I. M. Pei at the opening of the new
    Suzhou Museum
2   I. M. Pei on the construction site
3   Panoramic view of the Suzhou Museum

4

5, 6   View of the Suzhou Museum garden

5

6

A New Style for an Old Tradition

Pei's profound grasp of the local culture enabled him in the new museum to graft seamlessly a modern design onto classical Suzhou style. His design takes full cognizance of 2,500 years of Suzhou history and architecture, both in terms of domestic building and of the classical garden. Pei's building reflects the spirit of the old by translating its appearance into the new. The new building melts harmoniously into the urban texture of Suzhou. How did he realize this harmonious integration of innovation and tradition? The answer lies in the use of modern materials to recreate traditional structures and the adaptation of traditional building elements to create a fresh look.

The complexity of the new steel and glass roof recreates the distinctive characteristic of a seemingly random mixture of movement and structure to be found in traditional Suzhou architecture while the traditional pattern of white walls with black tiles is recreated by white walls with grey black granite: easy to maintain and resonating with even more colour and lustre. The contrast with the white walls is fresh, elegant and arresting.

7

Olive Green Lotus-Shaped Bowl from the 'Five Dynasties'

This Olive Green Lotus-shaped Bowl from the 'Five Dynasties' was one of the most precious collections in Suzhou Museum. It was discovered on the third level of the Yunyan Pagoda (Tiger Hill, Suzhou) in 1957. It is composed of a bowl and a saucer. The overall height is 13.5cm. The bowl is 8.9cm high and the diameter of its mouth is 13.9cm. The saucer is 6.6cm high, and the diameters of its mouth and bottom are 14.9cm and 9.3cm respectively.

The Bowl (Yue ware) has an upright mouth, deep belly and ring foot; the shape of the saucer is like dou, contracted waist. The mouth of the saucer is averted while the ring-foot flared. The bass-relief lotus-flower designs can be seen on the surface of the bowl, the face of the saucer, and the ring foot overlapping one another. The design is cunning and the shape is exquisite looking like a blooming lotus. Lotus is a popular theme in the writings of many Chinese scholars, and a spiritual symbol in Buddhism. The significance of the Lotus Bowl, as a piece of art cannot be measured by money. The primary color is porcelain white with a tinge of gray in fine texture. All tiny granules are identical and pure in quality. The glazing is so beautiful that it brings out a warm, jade-like feeling. It was recognized as the standard for the olive green porcelain in the 'Five Dynasties', North Song Dynasty, and recently classified as one of the national treasures by our government.

With regard to the texture and color of the olive green porcelain, experts from Qing Dynasty all agreed that the color was close to the Yue ware but its luster was even clearer. From some of the excavated olive green porcelain, it is observed that the texture is in very fine quality, and the color is a mix of gray and light gray. They have thin paste wall and smooth surface; with standardized shape and even glazing. In the early Five Dynasties, the glazing was primarily in the color of yellow, rather lustrous and translucent. In late Tang Dynasty, the use of bluish green was increasing. Therefore, the color stays primarily in bluish green instead of yellow.

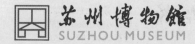
苏州博物馆
SUZHOU MUSEUM

Add:No.204,Dongbei Street,Suzhou
Tel:67575666 67575111
Fax:0512-67544232

Dong Ting Shan" Natural Mineral Water is the appointed drinking water of Suzhou Museum

五代秘色瓷莲花碗

五代秘色瓷莲花碗，国宝级文物，是苏州博物馆的珍贵馆藏之一。1957年在苏州虎丘云岩寺塔第三层的天宫中发现。它由碗和其下的盏托组合而成，通高13.5厘米，其中碗高8.9厘米、口径13.9厘米；盏托高6.6厘米、口径14.9厘米、底径9.3厘米。

这件越窑秘色瓷莲花碗，碗为直口深腹圈足；盏托形状如豆，盘口外翻，束腰，圈足外撇。碗身外壁、盏托盘面和圈足均饰重瓣莲花，如浅浮雕状突起。莲花碗构思巧妙，造型精致，端庄有姿，恰如一朵盛开的莲花。莲花是中国文人士大夫永恒的艺术主题，又是佛教中无比高尚的艺术象征，因而，此莲花碗的艺术造型与艺术价值是无与伦比的。从该器露胎处可见瓷胎呈灰白色，细腻致密，颗粒均匀纯净；特别是它的釉色滋润内敛，掠翠融青，呈现出玉一般的温润感，被公认为五代、北宋年间秘色瓷标准器。

所谓"秘色"，据宋人解释是：吴越国钱氏割据政权控制了越窑窑场，命令这些瓷窑专烧供奉用的瓷器，庶民不得使用，所以叫"秘色瓷"。如赵麟在《侯鲭录》中说："今之秘色瓷器，世言钱氏立国，越州烧进，为供奉之物，不得臣庶用之，故谓之秘色"。但有人认为，"秘色"并非神秘之"秘"，也不是统治阶级所专有的意思，而是当时人们对青瓷那种色样之统称，就像晋代称青瓷为缥瓷一样。而日本的古陶瓷研究者认为：秘色即翡色，秘与翡乃一音之转。

关于秘色瓷的质地和色泽，清人说是"其色似越器，而清亮过之"。从出土的典型的秘色瓷看，其质地细腻，原料的处理精细，多呈灰或浅灰色，胎壁较薄，表面光滑，器型规整，施釉均匀。从釉色来说，五代早期仍以黄为主，滋润光泽，呈半透明状，但青绿的比重较晚唐有所增加。其后便以青绿为主，黄色则不多见。

"洞庭山"天然泉水为苏州博物馆制定饮用水

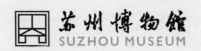

苏州博物馆
SUZHOU MUSEUM

地址:苏州市东北街204号
电话:67575666 67575111
传真:0512-67544232

苏州博物馆
SUZHOU MUSEUM

地址：苏州市东北街204号
ADD:No.204 Dongbei Street,Suzhou
电话/TEL: 0512-67575666 67575111
传真/FAX: 0512-67544232

2010/7/17—8/15   现代艺术厅 Contemporary Art Galleries

游子心·故乡情——严隽泰伉俪油画作品展
The Traveler Thinks Longingly of Home—The Paintings of Mr.and Mrs.T.T.Yen

"洞庭山"天然泉水为本次特展指定用水
Dong Ting Shan Natural Mineral Water is the appointed drinking water of Suzhou Museum

Mr. T.T. Yen, whose ancestral hometown is Mudu Town, Suzhou, and whose father is Mr. C.K. Yen, was born in Shanghai in 1936 and later moved to Taipei with his family.

The rich cultural education T.T. Yen received from his parents had a profound influence on him, and he has also been heavily influenced by his wife Grace Yen. An entrepreneur with a background in electrical engineering who has overseen major construction projects around the world, T.T. Yen did not commit himself to painting until the age of 60. He then became a joyful painter who "pays respect to color."

T.T. Yen, who is a self-taught painter, combines Chinese imagery with Western techniques. He spontaneously expresses his inner feelings on canvas, capturing illusory and abstract thoughts that reflect all the various emotions he has experienced in life. All of the colors in his paintings merge as if they were destined to do so. They flow, diverge, radiate, and blend, stretching proportionately to every inch of the painting. It is full of life and ever-changing, spilling forth like harmonious and splendid music.

T.T. Yen once said: "These paintings make me think of all the roads I have taken in my life. No matter how long the journey, you always start out rooted in your own culture. My hometown is Suzhou, and my unchanging starting point is always the beauty of Chinese culture that was passed down to me from my parents."

Grace Yen, born into a prominent family in Hsilo Township in Changhua County, Taiwan, started taking painting lessons from art educator Li Zhong-sheng from an early age, and then furthered her studies at Tokyo University of the Arts. While studying abroad in Japan, she went to Hong Kong many times to study under famous painter Liu Hai-su. Her many years of education in the field of painting have cultivated Grace Yen's rich professional artistic quality.

Grace Yen excels at the Toyoga painting style and oils, and she has a unique understanding of floral arrangement. Plants and flowers are the subjects in most of her works. She has a fresh, distinctive style of handling the textures of petals, stems, and leaves. Her paintings have gorgeous color schemes and exact structures that retain their simple, natural style. The painting scenes are peaceful and joyful, like the gentle nature of the painter.

Mr. and Mrs. Yen are a harmonious married couple, and though they are immersed in their artistic creations every day, one can always glimpse interaction between them in their brush strokes. It's just as T.T. Yen says, "There's no need for language between family members. We just naturally share aesthetic experiences and the tacit understanding of life in the home, in the garden, and in the spaces of our paintings." This shows the reserved nature of Chinese people, and it also reflects the special everyday aesthetics of Suzhou residents. Silence wins out over words, and art is inseparable from life. Moreover, art is a kind of communication on a deeper level.

This is the first painting exhibition from Taiwan to be held in the Suzhou Museum's new exhibition hall, and one of the exhibitors is also originally from Suzhou, which lends the event a special significance. Sincere thanks go out to all the people who made this exhibition possible.

2010/7/17——8/15

The Traveler Thinks Longingly of Home ——The Paintings of Mr.and Mrs.T.Yen

游子心 故乡情

严隽泰伉俪油画作品展

苏州博物馆现代艺术展厅
Contemporary Art Galleries

苏州博物馆
SUZHOU MUSEUM

地址：苏州市东北街204号
ADD:No.204 Dongbei Street,Suzhou
电话/TEL：0512-67575666 67575111
传真/FAX：0512-67544232

　　严隽泰先生，祖籍苏州木渎镇，是严家淦先生的公子，1936年生于上海，后举家迁往台北。

　　隽泰先生固家学渊源，自幼耳濡目染，加之夫人许婉瑱女士的影响敦促，这位走遍五大洲、负责过世界各地重大工程、以电机专业见长的企业家，60岁开始专心绘事，成为一位"向色彩致敬"的快乐画者。

　　隽泰先生以自画自学的方式，融合中国意象与西方技法，即兴自在地绘出内心的感受，甚而捕捉虚拟、抽象的思想，映现生命行旅的哀乐悲喜。其画作，所有的色彩都在因缘际会下聚集汇合，在画面上流动、析离、散放、消融，恰如其分地伸展至方寸画布的每个位置，生机盎然，变化处处，奏出和谐曼妙的乐章。

　　隽泰先生说："这些画令我想起曾经走过的千山万水。但旅程再远，仍是从自身文化的根底出发。故乡苏州，与先严先慈在生活中传达给我的中国文化之美，是我永远不变的起点。"

　　严夫人许婉瑱女士出生于台湾彰化的西螺望族，早年受前辈艺术教育家李仲生启蒙，及长赴东京大学深造。旅日期间又数度飞往香港，求教著名画家刘海粟先生。多年的绘画艺术历练，造就了婉瑱女士深厚的绘画专业素养。

　　婉瑱女士擅长东洋画风和油彩，更对花艺有独到的见解。她的作品中，最常以花卉为题，对于花瓣、枝叶的纹理，处理方式清新独到，设色绮丽、结构严谨却又不失朴拙自然之风，画面祥和喜悦，一如画家的温和性情。

　　严氏伉俪琴瑟和谐，平日各自沉浸在艺术创作里，却随时随地留下了对话的伏笔。正如隽泰先生所说："家人之间不用言语，而是自然地在屋宇、庭园和画面的空间中，分享美感的经验、生活的默契。"这既是中国人的含蓄，也有苏州人特殊的生活美学。此时无声胜有声，艺术不但没有远离生活，更是一种深层的交流。

　　这个展览是苏州博物馆新馆举办的第一个来自祖国宝岛台湾的画展，而画展的主人之一又是苏州人，画展自然多了一份特殊的意义。衷心感谢所有促成此次展览的人士。

Zhong Wang Fu's Restoration

Zhong Wang Fu (Prince Zhong's mansion) at Dongbei Street in Suzhou, a total area of 10,650 square meter, is the most complete historic architectural complex of the Taiping Heavenly Kingdom that has been preserved in China. The entire complex with two floors can be divided into the central, eastern and western sections.

Zhong Wang Fu was originally built by Prince Zhong, Li Xiucheng, during September 1860 to December 1863 and based partially on Humble Administrator's Garden and its eastern and western residences. After the Taiping Heavenly Kingdom failed, it became Li Hongzhang's residence when he was Jiangsu Provincial Governor. Although partially destroyed by Qing Army, its scale and basic structure were preserved. Suzhou Museum based on it was opened to public On January 1st, 1960. In 1961, it was classified as the National Priority Preservative Unit of the Cultural Relics by the State Council.

In order to protect its historical significance and art value, the mansion was repaired seven times from 1951 to 1975. Since 1980s, repair was also made to the gate, the ceremonial door, two verandas, the main, the rear and the second hall. In 1993, the repair of the middle and east section was completed with funds from the State Administration of Cultural Heritage. In 2006, the newly repaired Zhong Wang Fu is opened as a part of New Suzhou Museum.

Zhong Wang Fu houses a number of Taiping cultural relics such as vivid stone lions and color paintings on the beams, as well as a Chinese wistaria planted by Wen Zhengming and a classical opera stage. The eastern section exhibits the restoration of the Fengzhi Guild Hall of the Eight Banners; the north displays the cultural relics donated by Mr. Zhang Zongxian; the west is restored into Zhang Luqian's houses and part of Buyuan Garden, as well as a library of ancient books.

The exhibitions of Zhong Wang Fu are concentrated in its central section. Prince Zhong's early career achievements are showed in the eastern veranda and the making of Sufu province is in the western one. Cultural relics and historical documents on policies and regime of the Taiping Heavenly Kingdom are in the main hall that also has been restored to the scenes when Prince Zhong held military meetings. Foreign trade of Sufu province is showed in the eastern wing-room, and historical materials found in Suzhou are exhibited in the western. Prince Zhong's three-time attacks on Shanghai, Fight for Suzhou, his death and relative works are displayed in the second hall.

苏州博物馆
SUZHOU MUSEUM

Add:No.204,Dongbei Street,Suzhou
Tel:67575666 67575111
Fax:0512-67544232

太平天国忠王府旧址陈列

太平天国忠王府旧址位于苏州市东北街，占地面积10650平方米，建筑面积7500平方米，是全国保存至今最完整的一组集公署、住宅、园林于一体的太平天国历史建筑群。建筑群座北朝南，分成中、东、西三部分，以地面一层为主，局部二层，雄伟壮丽，错落曲折。

忠王府为太平天国忠王李秀成在1860年9月至1863年12月期间，利用原拙政园花园部分及东西部宅第等合并改建而成，它是太平天国在苏浙地区的最高统帅府。太平天国运动失败后，忠王府成为李鸿章的江苏巡抚行辕，他曾感慨忠王府"平生所未见之境也"。忠王府虽然遭到清军的一些破坏，但其建筑规模和基本格局都保存了下来。1960年元旦，苏州博物馆在忠王府旧址建筑群正式对外开放。1961年被国务院公布为第一批全国重点文物保护单位。1996年被确认为"中国现存太平天国王府中最完美的建筑"，并因此入选"1949—1995中华之最"。

忠王府旧址不仅存有浑厚朴实的龙凤纹饰窗棂和神态生动的石狮等太平天国时期珍贵遗物，还保存有太平天国400余幅秀丽典雅的苏式梁枋彩绘，9幅清新隽秀的彩绘壁画，其数量之多、艺术水平之高，全国罕见。此外，这里还有明代文徵明手植紫藤等名木植物和江南最大的室内古戏台。

为妥善保护这座具有历史意义和艺术价值的建筑，1951年至1975年，曾对其官署部分7次修缮，80年代又陆续将大门、仪门、两庑、大殿、后堂、二殿等作了全面维修，基本上恢复了忠王府官署建筑的原貌。1993年起，由国家文物局拨款，完成了中路官署建筑和东路部分宅第建筑的修复，使其更显宏伟。2006年，修葺一新的忠王府作为苏州博物馆新馆的组成部分，正以崭新的面貌迎接八方宾客，成为苏州一处独特的人文景观。

忠王府旧址的东路，以恢复晚清八旗奉直会馆原貌为主。利用北部四面厅以专题形式举办《香港张宗宪先生捐赠文物陈列》，以纪念和表彰张宗宪先生对家乡文化遗产保护事业的支持。忠王府旧址的西路，则以恢复清光绪年间张履谦豪宅及补园部分建筑原貌为主，北部的小姐楼作为博物馆的藏书楼。

太平天国忠王府旧址陈列主要集中在中路展出，东庑为忠王李秀成早期征战事迹陈列。西庑为苏福省建设陈列。大殿恢复忠王李秀成主持军事会议的场景以及有关政策制度方面的文物史料陈列。东厢房为太平天国苏福省对外贸易陈列。西厢房为苏州发现的一批太平天国史料文献陈列。二殿主要陈列李秀成三次征战上海、苏州保卫战、忠王之死以及相关纪念作品等。通过这些文物、照片、史料等，人们可以了解并研究李秀成以及太平天国苏福省那段逝去了的历史。

"洞庭山"天然泉水为苏州博物馆制定饮用水

苏州博物馆 SUZHOU MUSEUM

地址:苏州市东北街204号
电话:67575666　67575111
传真:0512-67544232

The Exhibition of Zhang Zongxian

Zhang Zongxian(Robert Chang), is a great master in the cultural relic collection and auction circles at home and abroad. He is now a member of standing committee of Suzhou Municipal Political Consultative Conference, consultant of Suzhou Museum, deputy chairman of Suzhou Association of Hong Kong, and consultants of many cultural relics and arts auction companies such as China Guardian Auctions, Hanhai Auction, Rongbaozhai and Duoyunxuan. His legend has also been widely talked about in the circle.

Zhang Zongxian was born in Suzhou, Jiangsu. His grandfather, Zhang Yiru, was an authority in bamboo carvings, and his father, Zhang Zhongying, was outstanding in Shanghai antique circle. Zhang, the first person attending international auction from Hong Kong, China, has entered the field when young. For half a century, Zhang has made great efforts in developing Hong Kong to a Chinese antique and arts trade center.

Zhang Zongxian always loves Chinese cultural relics and tries his best to protect them. For carrying forward Chinese culture and enriching the national arts, he donated 180 porcelains and 44 painting and calligraphy works, which were scattered overseas and privately collected by him for many years to Suzhou Museum, in November 1992 and October 1993 respectively. Mr. Zhang has always been concerned and supportive to the development of Suzhou Museum. His fervent love for his country and hometown, and his selfless donation has earned people's respect and admiration.

Suzhou, paradise of the world, is a famous historic and cultural city. It has many precious cultural relics, scenic spots, and historical sites left by ancients. It is a witness of history, a symbol of civilization, and the fortune of people. Mr. Zhang's donation to his hometown has added luster to this ancient city.

In a special cultural relics exhibition of Zhang Zongxian's donations, Suzhou Museum exhibits these porcelains and paintings and calligraphy in a long term to commemorate and commend Mr. Zhang for his support to the cultural heritage protection of his hometown. Besides, another seven exquisite porcelains offered by him specially for the opening of New Suzhou Museum will be exhibited for one year.

苏州博物馆
SUZHOU MUSEUM

Add:No.204,Dongbei Street,Suzhou
Tel:67575666 67575111
Fax:0512-67544232

Dong Ting Shan" Natural Mineral Water is the appointed drinking water of Suzhou Museum

香港张宗宪先生捐赠文物陈列

张宗宪(Robret Chang)，是一位在中国香港、台湾、内地乃至世界文物收藏界和拍卖界享誉极高的大家，现为苏州市政协常委、苏州博物馆顾问、香港苏州同乡会副会长，身兼中国嘉德、北京翰海、北京荣宝斋、上海朵云轩等多家著名文物艺术品拍卖公司顾问。

张宗宪系苏州人，祖父张揖如为近代竹刻巨擘，父亲张仲英为上海古董界翘楚。张宗宪早年入行，成为第一个出现在国际拍卖会上的中国香港人。半个世纪以来，香港发展成中国文物艺术交易中心，与他的努力密不可分。

张宗宪对于中国文物呵护倍加，情有独钟。多年来，张宗宪先生对苏州博物馆的发展一直十分关心，为弘扬祖国灿烂文化，丰富华夏民族艺术宝库，满怀对祖国、对家乡的深情厚意，分别于1992年11月和1993年10月将多年精心收藏曾流失海外的瓷器180件、书画44件捐赠给苏州博物馆。这种慷慨捐赠、无私奉献之举，令人钦佩。

捐赠瓷器中，有汉代的绿釉陶牧圈、农舍；晋代的越窑青釉贴花双耳盖壶；唐代的白釉器、黑釉器；宋代的耀州、影青、龙泉等名窑瓷器；元代的龙泉青瓷铁斑双耳瓶；明代的永乐白釉高足杯、嘉靖五彩花碟缸等。清代瓷器更是绚丽多彩，有素三彩、粉彩、珐琅彩、古铜彩、吉翠釉、青花釉里红、胭脂红、开片青釉、天蓝釉、木纹釉、茶叶末釉、蓝釉、法华釉、黄釉等。此外玉器中有乾隆白玉长方几、红玉双耳扁方瓶。铜器中有唐镜、鎏金铜三宝佛等。另外，还有14K金镶钻石翡翠纸镇、近代桃花红晶雕刘海戏蟾像、中国刑法图一套及班禅额尔德尼题赠藏文水墨红绢本立轴等，均极具收藏价值。

捐赠书画中，有清代著名金石书法家赵之谦的《如松之茂图》、张大千的《山水图》、清雍正皇帝像、嘉庆皇帝御笔诗、李鸿章对联、敦煌壁画以及吴昌硕的《葡萄》、陈半丁的《花卉》、陆廉夫的《金纸花卉》等珍贵作品。

张宗宪先生两次慷赠文物、惠泽故里的行动，为苏州这座历史文化名城又增添了新的光彩。为此，苏州博物馆以《香港张宗宪先生捐赠文物陈列》的专题展览形式，在忠王府四面厅长期陈列展出这批捐赠文物，以纪念和表彰张宗宪先生对家乡文化遗产保护事业的支持。同时，在新馆展室开辟专柜展出1年张宗宪先生友情提供的7件瓷器精品。

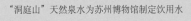
"洞庭山"天然泉水为苏州博物馆制定饮用水

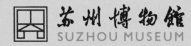
苏州博物馆
SUZHOU MUSEUM

地址：苏州市东北街204号
电话：67575666 67575111
传真：0512-67544232

I. M. Pei and the New Suzhou Museum

In today's modern architecture, undoubtedly Mr. I. M. Pei has earned himself a distinguished position as one of the most renowned architects in the world. In fact, being the only architect with a Chinese origin, made him even more unique in the 21st century.

Mr. Pei was born in Guangzhou on April 26, 1917. His ancestors had been a prominent family in Suzhou. So he spent a few years of his childhood in his family's estate, namely, the Lion Forest Garden, in Suzhou. Mr. Pei said, "It did have an influence on my work."

Mr. Pei has designed museums, college buildings, commercial centers and many skyscrapers. With his innovation and creativity, he built many extraordinary buildings all over the world, in Canada, France, Germany, Australia, Japan, Singapore, Iran and Taiwan. In 1983, Pei was awarded the Pritzker Architecture Prize. Even at this stage, he continues to pursue his dreams and surpass himself by making his design highly monumental than ever. He is truly an outstanding architect by trade.

The new Museum designed by Mr. Pei was completed in October 2006, covering over 10,700 square meters and located at the cross section of Dongbei Street and Qimen Road. It is divided into three main areas. The center area includes the entrance, the hall and the garden while the West Wing covers the exhibition area. In the East Wing, located there are the administration offices and education facilities. The layout of the three axes matches the style of Prince Zhong's Mansion. The typical colors of the whitewashed plaster wall, and the dark gray clay tile, used in the traditional constructions all over Suzhou, are adopted by the new Museum as the primary colors. However, instead of using traditional clay tiles, Mr. Pei had the roof replaced by gray granites. The modern steel structure is applied to the new Museum in place of the traditional roof beams. The interior is constructed with wooden frames and white ceiling. In addition, metal sunscreens with wooden panels are introduced to bring in more lights, and make the Museum look even more sophisticated.

Under the design concept of "Chinese style with innovation, Suzhou style with creativity" and the idea of "not too high, not too large and not too abrupt", the Museum was built to be a modern, artistic and comprehensive museum in terms of its selected site, and quality construction. Not only does it have the characteristics of a garden of Suzhou style, but also contains the simple geometric balance of the modern art as well as the exquisite structural layout in full function. The construction of the new Museum makes excellent use of spaces for the Museum to educate visitors on the subjects of culture, history and art. The fact that it is adjacent to a few classical gardens, such as the Humble Administrator's Garden, Zhong Wang Fu and the Lion Forest Garden, makes it become a historical, art and cultural complex within a few blocks, enriching one another.

The new Suzhou Museum is said to be the last design of Mr. I. M. Pei in his career. Therefore, not only does it become a monumental building in Suzhou, but also a significant construction, merging the traditional Chinese architectural design with the future. It enhances the protection of Suzhou cultural heritages, and enables Suzhou Museum to turn on a new page.

苏州博物馆
SUZHOU MUSEUM

Add:No.204,Dongbei Street,Suzhou
Tel:67575666 67575111
Fax:0512-67544232

Dong Ting Shan" Natural Mineral Water is the appointed drinking water of Suzhou Museum

贝聿铭与苏州博物馆新馆

在当代建筑设计领域中，贝聿铭是世界范围内最为公众熟知的建筑大师，是跻身于世界级建筑师行列的唯一华人，被誉为20世纪最重要的建筑艺术家之一。

贝聿铭1917年4月26日出生于广州，祖辈是苏州望族，童年时曾在家族拥有的苏州园林狮子林度过一段时光。20世纪30年代中期，贝聿铭负笈美国学习建筑学。在几十年的建筑设计生涯中，不仅在美国设计过许

多博物馆、学院、商业中心、摩天大厦等，还在加拿大、法国、德国、澳大利亚、日本、新加坡、伊朗和中国北京、香港、台湾等地设计过不少大型公共建筑。贝聿铭在世界各地的建筑作品达70余项，获各类奖项50余次。1983年，贝聿铭获得了被称为建筑界诺贝尔奖的"普利茨克奖"。对梦想的执着追求和对自身的不断超越，使众多贝氏建筑成为不朽的经典之作。

苏州博物馆新馆是国内唯一一座由贝聿铭亲自设计的博物馆，位于苏州东北街和齐门路相汇处，占地面积约10700平方米、建筑面积19000余平方米，2006年10月竣工开馆。新馆包括修葺一新的太平天国忠王府，总建筑面积26500平方米，和毗邻的拙政园、狮子林等园林名胜形成了一条丰富多彩的历史文化长廊。

新馆建筑群座北朝南，分为三大区域：中部为入口、前庭、中央大厅和主庭院；西部为博物馆主展区；东部为辅展区和行政办公区。这种以中轴线对称的东、中、西三路布局与忠王府格局相互映衬，十分和谐。为充分尊重所在街区的历史风貌，新馆采用地下一层、地面一层为主，主体建筑檐口高度控制在6米之内，中央大厅和西部展厅设计了局部二层，高度16米，未超出周边古建筑的最高点。正门对面的步行街南侧为河畔小广场，杨柳依依，桃花灿灿。广场两侧修复了古色古香的沿街古建筑，集书画、工艺、茶楼、小吃等公众配套服务于一体。

新馆色调以传统的粉墙黛瓦为基本元素，在错落有致的建筑布局中，用色泽更为均匀的深灰色石材做屋面和墙体边饰，与白墙相配，清新雅洁，给江南建筑符号增加了新的诠释内涵。在建筑构造上，屋面形态的设计突破了中国传统建筑"大屋顶"在采光方面的束缚，玻璃、开放式钢结构可以让室内借到大片天光。新馆还有园艺的创新，造景设计从古典园林的精髓中提炼而出，由池塘、假山、小桥、亭台、竹林等组成的创意山水园与传统园林有机结合，创造性地延续了一代名园拙政园。

苏州博物馆新馆以其意味深长的精准选址，体现"中而新、苏而新"的设计理念、追求"不高不大不突出"的设计原则，成为一座既有苏州传统建筑特色又有现代建筑艺术风格的现代化博物馆。它不仅是当今苏州的一个标志性公共建筑，也是中国建筑文化从传统走向未来的一座桥梁，更为苏州博物馆的传承与创新翻开了崭新一页。

"洞庭山"天然泉水为苏州博物馆制定饮用水

苏州博物馆
SUZHOU MUSEUM

地址：苏州市东北街204号
电话：67575666 67575111
传真：0512-67544232

I. M. Pei and the New Suzhou Museum

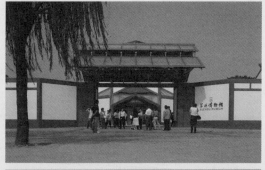

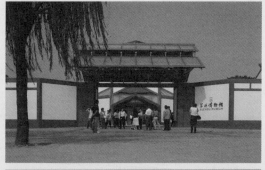

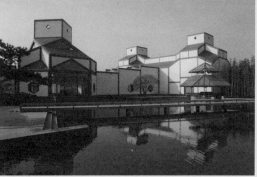

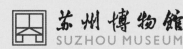

Pearl Pillar of the Buddhist Shrine

The Pearl Pillar of the Buddhist Shrine, a very precious Buddhist artwork, that was dated back nearly thousand years from now, was created in Northern Song Dynasty. This creation combined various Chinese traditional craftwork techniques such as carving, painting with gold lines, weaving with gold and silver thread, and jewelry inlay craftsmanship etc. A combination of such work is rare as it displays ingenuity, rich connotation, expensive materials, and excellence in craftsmanship. It is regarded as a rarity of Northern Song Dynasty, and was classified as the national treasure in 1993.

In 1978, three kids accidentally found the valuable Buddhist relics in Suzhou Ruiguang Pagoda. Among several ancient engraved sutras and pieces of handicrafts, the Pearl Pillar of the Buddhist Shrine is the most appealing of the excavation.

The structure of Pearl Pillar of the Buddhist Shrine is ingenious. Its design embodies Buddhism's view of the world, and their grand mythical world. The overall height of Pearl Pillar of the Buddhist Shrine is 122.6cm. It consists of three sections: the Buddhist Mount Sumeru, Dhvaja, and Finial. The base, the Buddhist Mount Sumeru, is an octagon-shaped platform representing the Buddhism's eight-phased-sky. There are three layers of the Buddhist Mount Sumeru. Each layer consists of 8 sides; each corner are covered with different lacquer patterns and surrounded with 8 silver lions. The cinnabar lacquer relic in gold tracery gives us the impression of the profound respect for Buddhism.

The top portion of the base is a platform, surrounded with sandalwood carving techniques. In the middle of the Buddhist Mount Sumeru, this mushroom-like mountain is surrounded by sea, which implies Buddhism's 9 mountains and 8 seas. Above the sea level there are 8 auspicious clouds, and on top of them stand Four Devarajas (heavenly guardians) and Four Apsaras beside them. In addition, there are Eight Tutelaries on the top carved with sandalwood; the legendary deities of Buddhism.

The Dhvaja is surrounded by 8 pillars and covered by a roof, which are woven by gold-and-silver threads. There are also many pearls and gems embellished on the top of the roof. The Buddhist Canopy sitting above is stringed with jewelry. At the head of the Buddhist Canopy, there is a translucent crystal symbolizing the purity of Buddhism.

Nowadays this exquisite piece of art is like a luminous pearl shining uniquely over this beautiful, ancient, and civilized city, Suzhou.

苏州博物馆
SUZHOU MUSEUM

Add:No.204,Dongbei Street,Suzhou
Tel:67575666 67575111
Fax:0512-67544232

Dong Ting Shan" Natural Mineral Water is the
appointed drinking water of Suzhou Museum

真珠舍利宝幢

真珠舍利宝幢，国宝级文物，是苏州博物馆馆藏珍贵文物之一，1978年在苏州瑞光寺塔第三层天宫中发现，为北宋遗物，距今一千年左右。宝幢主体用楠木构成，分为须弥座、须弥山海、幢殿、刹四部分，通高122.6厘米。

须弥座：包括牙脚八棱台座、宝山与大海等部分。台座呈八棱形，每一棱角底部有燕尾形牙脚。八棱台座分三层，中间束腰部位一周设24个壸门；中间层阶上置8只小银狮，造型生动；银狮内侧八棱斜弧面一周贴饰有堆漆描金制成的16个供养人形象。其上平阶一周置8只立体雕刻的小木狮；平阶内侧收腰处镂如意壸门，上承环绕勾栏。八根栏柱顶端，缀银丝串珠莲花，莲花上各置一颗水晶球。须弥座造型极为精美繁复，通体描绘宝相、缠枝、几何图案，细如纤毫。

须弥山海：勾栏平阶之内，一周立面及圆形平面上雕出浪涛滚滚的大海，整体描金；海浪周边雕出向上升腾而起的8朵描金祥云，云顶端立有4男4女共8位天神；大海中央如蘑菇云般突起透雕的山柱，柱上盘绕一条鎏金银丝串珠编织而成的九头蟠龙，圆柱上端托起由16座叠嶂山峦组成的须弥山。

幢殿：系真珠舍利宝幢的中间部分，居须弥宝山之上。幢殿由殿基、殿柱、殿外护法八天、八棱经幢、幢顶鎏金银龛、殿顶、漆木龛、华盖等部分组成。一周8根殿柱，均由镶包鎏金银丝的细木柱制成，下置覆莲状水晶柱础，柱础之下刻有云雾缭绕的殿基；殿柱外侧一周，有神情各异的护法八天木雕。殿内中部立有宝蓝色八棱柱状经幢，经幢八面依次以真（楷）、草、隶、篆书阴刻填金七佛之名，及梵语"南无摩诃般若波罗密"（意为"大智慧可达彼岸乐土"）；幢体中空，内置淡青色葫芦形玻璃小瓶一个，瓶内藏舍利子9颗。另置梵文和汉文经咒各1页，钱币16枚，银龙2条，印章1枚以及结晶矿石数捻块。幢顶置有缠枝纹鎏金银皮小龛，一尊木雕高僧大德祖师像跌坐其间。殿柱及幢顶鎏金银龛之上为圆形八出殿顶，横梁、斗拱、瓦片、滴水等皆用粗银丝为骨，细银丝网结，串以珍珠；梁角处还有8只护梁神形象；所有斗拱梁枋、飞椽出戗，均缀串密集的小珍珠；八出戗角端部悬垂有宝花璎珞幡铎。殿顶之上又置有堆漆描金宝相花纹木龛，龛内盛放金雕细颈宝瓶，宝瓶的金纯度为98.5%。木龛上复置八角形金银丝串珠华盖，华盖周边缀有红、蓝、白等各色宝珠，华盖上还饰有8条串珠天龙，呈放射状沿华盖顶间向下昂首俯冲，使华盖和其下的殿顶如同八脊重檐翘角般富丽堂皇。

刹：系真珠舍利宝幢上层部分，立于幢殿华盖之上。主体呈柱状，由银棒和包金箔木柱相接而成，刹轮以白玉、水晶、五色料珠等制成，间以金银绞花、叶片及银丝串珠装饰；刹轮上部为银丝串珠小幡盖，小幡盖一周垂8条流苏银链，下接华盖八角；刹顶部为水晶质摩尼宝珠，直径3.4厘米，宝珠两侧以银丝挽出火焰光造型，以示"瑞光普照"。

真珠舍利宝幢造型之优美、选材之名贵、工艺之精巧，举世罕见。制作者根据佛教中所说的世间"七宝"，选取名贵的水晶、玛瑙、琥珀、珍珠、檀香木、金、银等材料，运用了玉石雕刻、金银丝编制、金银皮雕刻、檀香木雕、水晶雕、堆漆、描金、贴金箔、穿珠、彩绘等十多种特种工艺技法精心制作，巧夺天工，精美绝世。如宝幢上装饰的珍珠就达3万多颗；17尊木雕的神像更见功力，每尊佛像仅高约10厘米，雕刻难度极大；天王的威严神态，天女的婀娜多姿，护法八天的嗔怒神情，祖师大德的静穆庄严，均雕得出神入化。真珠舍利宝幢体现了苏州工艺美术的繁荣和精美，同时也可见北宋时期吴人高度的审美水准和丰富的文化内涵。

苏州博物馆
SUZHOU MUSEUM

地址:苏州市东北街204号
电话:67575666 67575111
传真:0512-67544232

"洞庭山"天然泉水为苏州博物馆制定饮用水

In ancient China, the 'Guanzhong' area in The Tang tricolor pottery, more commonly known as 'Tang San Cai', is a popular name for the multi-color potteries fired by relatively low temperature. They were originated from the single-color pottery of the Hang and Wei Dynasties and further enhanced by the craftsmen in Tang Dynasty. The colors of the glaze include yellow, green, white, brown, blue and black, while the dominant colors are yellow, green and white. We therefore had named it the Tang- tricolor-pottery. The earliest 'Tang San Cai' was excavated in the City of Luoyang, also from there were the largest number of potteries ever discovered so far. Therefore, people nicknamed it as 'Luoyang-Tang-tricolor-pottery'. The method of making such a colorful pottery is to mix various metallic oxides into the glaze. The metallic oxides emerges different colors during the firing process. The colors are blended with one another to reflect a natural color, or merged color, or multi-colors which provide a very unique, colorful and splendid charm to the Tang tricolor pottery.

Tang Dynasty is generally recognized as one of the most powerful dynasties in the Chinese history as evidenced by its splendid achievements in many areas, including culture, politics, economy and diplomacy. People at the time were in great pursuit of "living a life of luxury and dying with an elaborate funeral". Such type of pottery was the end-product of this extravagant practice. 'Tang San Cai' pottery thus became a milestone in the Chinese multicolor pottery development. It also had tremendous influence on the color-glazed pottery art in later stage as well as all over the world. Consequently, it inspired the creation of the Liao and Jin tricolor pottery and the Japanese Nara tricolor pottery. Through the Silk Road, the 'Tang San Cai' potteries were exported to the countries in West Asia, North Africa and along the Mediterranean coastal. Obviously, 'Tang San Cai' played a significant role in promoting the development of the color-glazed pottery art in the Western countries.

The city of Luoyang was designated as the eastern capital during Sui and Tang Dynasties and, as the Holy Capital under Wu Zetian's monarch. It was also the eastern starting point of the Silk Road. At the time, Luoyang was a grand city enjoyed great prosperity and international fame. Mount Mang, to the north of the Luoyang city, was viewed as the perfect deific graveyard with best 'Funshui'. So, many nobles, wealthy people and celebrities all wanted to build their tombs there. In 1905, the first piece of 'Tang San Cai' pottery was excavated from a ruined Tang Dynasty tomb. Since then, this type of magnificent pottery has become the gem of the ancient Chinese art work and, been favored by the researchers and antique collectors. So far, the excavated 'Tang San Cai' potteries has been numbered more than thousands, many of which are in excellent quality.

The government of Tang Dynasty set up a few special workshops for the production of the tricolor pottery in Gongyi and Huangye, all in Henan Province. The production began in early Tang Dynasty and peaked throughout the reigning periods of Gao Zong, Wu Zetian and Xuan Zong. The designing of the pottery fell into three primary categories; human figures, animals and utensils. The human figure and animal potteries are various in types, and vivid in expressions with perfect proportion and fine cuts. The utensil potteries are generally round and full, in mellow and rich colors truly reflecting the charm and style of Tang Dynasty. As viewers, we would be led to a fantasy; emerging ourselves to the ancient time long ago, and dreaming of the splendid Tang Dynasty far away.

We would like to give our gratitude to Luoyang Museum. Only with their active support, will we have the opportunity of stepping into a dream world of more than 1,000-year-old.

主办：苏州博物馆 洛阳博物馆

大唐遗韵 盛世华彩

洛阳出土唐三彩菁华展

苏州博物馆
SUZHOU MUSEUM

地址：苏州市东北街204号
ADD:No.204 Dongbei Street,Suzhou
电话/TEL： 0512-67575666 67575111
传真/FAX： 0512-67544232

2010/7/1—9/5 特展厅
Special Exhibition Gallery

Selected Tri-color potteries of Tang Dynasty unearthed from Luo Yang City

　　唐三彩是唐代工匠在汉魏单色釉陶基础上创新发展起来的低温多彩釉陶新品系的总称，釉彩有黄、绿、白、褐、蓝、黑等色，而以黄、绿、白三色为主，故习称唐三彩。因唐三彩最早、最多出土于洛阳，亦有"洛阳唐三彩"之称。其呈色机理是在色釉中加入不同的金属氧化物，经过焙烧，釉色在器表上互相侵润、自相映发，或原色或复色或兼色，故具斑驳绚丽、丰腴莹润、富丽堂皇的艺术魅力。

　　唐朝是世界公认的中国最强盛的时代之一，在文化、政治、经济、外交等方面都有辉煌的成就，时风"生则极养，死则厚葬"，故唐三彩的出现，是那个时代追求奢靡华美之风的产物，同时也成为了我国多彩釉陶发展的里程碑。唐三彩对后世和世界彩釉艺术的发展影响深远。唐三彩之后又产生了"辽三彩"、"金三彩"以及日本的"奈良三彩"、朝鲜半岛的"新罗三彩"。唐三彩沿着陆海"丝绸之路"也往西亚、北非和地中海沿岸，对西方彩釉艺术的发展起到了积极推动作用。

　　洛阳是隋唐时期的东都、武则天时期的神都、丝绸之路的东方起点，彼时喧嚣繁荣，是具有国际影响力的大都会。洛阳城北横亘东西的邙山，历来被神化为升遐天堂的风水宝地，成为皇室贵族、名流富贾殁后营造冥府之所。"北邙山上列坟茔，万古千秋对洛城"就是对邙山古墓离离的真实写照。清光绪三十一年（1905年）陇海铁路修至洛阳北邙段，从破坏的唐墓中首次发现了唐三彩，唐三彩从此惊艳于世，备受国内外古器物研究者的重视和古玩商的垂青。之后，洛阳地区不断有唐三彩出土，数量之多、质量之美，令人惊叹。目前经考古发掘的唐三彩达数千件（组）。

　　唐朝官府在河南巩义黄冶设置有专门制作唐三彩的作坊。唐三彩初始作，以高宗、武则天至玄宗时期为鼎盛，大体上可分为人物、动物和器物三种类别。人物俑和动物俑造型丰富多彩，雕刻和捏塑比例准确，线条流畅，生动传神，富有生活气息；器物类形体圆润饱满，釉色腴润富丽，如梦似幻、引人入胜，均艺术地再现了大唐盛世的风韵，令观者不禁有睹物怀古、览物兴情、"梦回唐朝"之感慕。

　　感谢洛阳市博物馆的友情合作，从而给我们带来如此美好如梦的感慕。

"洞庭山"天然泉水为本次特展指定用水　Dong Ting Shan Natural Mineral Water is the appointed drinking water of Suzhou Museum

The new Suzhou Museum

For 46 years since it was founded, Suzhou Museum has collected more than 30,000 cultural relics through many channels. Among them, approximately 250 are classified as national grade-one treasures, 1,100 national grade-two and 13,000 national grade-three. The museum is well known for its unearthed relics, paintings and

calligraphy of Ming and Qing Dynasties, seals, ancient arts and crafts. Its overall collection is rated only behind the collection of Nanjing Museum in Jiangsu Province. Not only do these art treasures tell the stories about the landscapes and people from the more contemporary Suzhou, but also emerge the life style and historical context of the ancient Suzhou.

On October 6th, 2006, the new Suzhou Museum, designed by I.M. Pei, was opened to the public. The building complex of the new Suzhou Museum is divided into three major parts. The center part includes the entrance, front court and great hall while the west wing is designated as the main exhibition area, and the east belongs to, primarily the administration offices and sub-exhibition galleries.

The total exhibition area covers roughly 3,600 square meters, and houses 1,160 cultural relics dated from the prehistoric era to Ming and Qing Dynasties as well as more recent years. The main exhibition area contains four permanent exhibits: Lost Treasures from Kingdom of Wu, National Treasures discovered from Ruiguang Pagoda, the Legacies from the Region of Middle Wu, and last but not least, Paintings and Calligraphy from the distinguished Wu School.

At the north of the first floor, stands a thatched Song Pavilion, which is also a special exhibit. It is a duplication of a scholar's studio from Song Dynasty, depicting a simple but natural style.

The gallery under the ground level is designated to occasionally display collections from other museums in China, and around the world. To celebrate the grand opening of the Museum, The painting of 'Prosperous Gusu Region', a well-known masterpiece, was on display for a month. It was the first time ever being shown in Suzhou upon its completion 247 years ago.

Through the corridor on the east wing, a sub-exhibition area is located. At the end of the corridor, you will find the Wistaria court and the coffee/tea house. Located on each side of the corridor, there are the library, the VIP room, the Museum shop and the contemporary art galleries. The contemporary art exhibits, either from the local artists or overseas, will be held here from time to time. For the grand opening celebration of the new Museum, art works of Zao Wou-Ki, Cai Guoqiang and Xu Bing are on display to the public. There was no precedence of the exhibition as grand as such in Suzhou. It was indeed an art festival ever offered to the Suzhou public by a group of top overseas Chinese artists, truly a tremendous treat.

苏州博物馆
SUZHOU MUSEUM

Add:No.204,Dongbei Street,Suzhou
Tel:67575666 67575111
Fax:0512-67544232

苏州博物馆新馆陈列

苏州博物馆新馆座北朝南，建筑群分为三大区域：中部为入口、前庭、中央大厅和主庭院；西部为博物馆主展区；东部为辅展区和行政办公区。

文物是博物馆业务活动的物质基础，苏州博物馆目前文物藏品约3万余件，其中国家一级文物近250件，二级文物1100余件，三级文物13000余件，尤以书画、瓷器以及明清工艺品优称于同级博物馆。这些人类活动的历史见证体现着文化苏州的风貌与个性，反映着古城苏州的品位与风格，是文明记忆的汇聚、凝练和传承。

苏州博物馆新馆文物展示面积3600平方米，文物展品1160余件（组），上起远古时期，下至明清及近现代，多为历代佳作和精品。西部主展区设有吴地遗珍、吴塔国宝、吴中风雅、吴门书画等四个富有苏州地方特色的系列基本陈列。地面一层悬臂式楼梯口两旁，各有一个如同八角塔身内部造型的展室，展出"吴塔国宝"系列文物，分别为虎丘云岩寺塔佛教文物陈列和瑞光寺塔佛教文物陈列，这批塔中瑰宝充溢着圣洁的宗教情怀，如昨夜星辰，依然烁烁生辉。地面一层南侧的"吴地遗珍"系列文物蕴涵深邃，元气淋漓，包括史前陶器、玉器；春秋青铜器、玉器；六朝青瓷、五代秘色瓷；元娘娘墓、明王锡爵墓随葬品等主题展室。一层北部的"吴中风雅"系列文物千姿百态，玲珑剔透，包括明书斋陈设、瓷器、玉器、竹木牙角器、文具、赏玩杂件、民俗小摆设、织绣服饰、宋画斋陈设等主题展室。设在主展区二层的"吴门书画"系列展室，以典藏书画精品展示为主导。地下特展厅将不定期举办海内外各博物馆的珍贵文物展览以飨观众，开馆庆典期间展出的是清代徐扬长卷巨作《姑苏繁华图》。这是该图在苏州绘制完成后，经过247年首次回到故乡与观众见面。

宋画斋是新馆中唯一以传统手法营造的展厅。茅草屋顶的宋画斋是一间复原的宋代民居厅堂，从基础到屋顶全部采用传统工艺，建筑材料也多为青石、编竹夹泥墙、梓木、茅草等传统建材。如屋顶是用一种生长在苏北沼泽地的红茅草铺就而成，经过处理可20年不腐，庭院中的石桌取自天然灵璧石，室内陈设着仿宋的家具与仿宋的书画。宋画斋体现了"简单、朴素、自然"的美丽，反映了贝聿铭"在一个现代化的建筑物上，体现出中国民族建筑艺术的精华"的设计思想，他要让这间茅庐本身成为展品，展示中国传统的建筑艺术。

通过中央大厅东侧的天窗廊道进入东部辅展区，廊道尽头设紫藤园和休憩茶室。南北两侧设有图书馆、贵宾厅、博物馆商店和现代艺术展厅等公共空间。贝聿铭认为，书画艺术在苏州有深厚的渊源与基础，让参观者看过古代的再看看现代的，使人感受中国书画艺术的连绵延续。开馆庆典期间现代艺术厅展出绘画大师赵无极、现代艺术家蔡国强、徐冰的作品，这个国内空前的展览是一次世界顶级华人艺术家联袂奉献给苏州人民的艺术盛宴。

"洞庭山"天然泉水为苏州博物馆制定饮用水

苏州博物馆
SUZHOU MUSEUM

地址:苏州市东北街204号
电话:67575666 67575111
传真:0512-67544232

7 The gateway
8 The entrance building

8

9,   Detail of the façade
10, 11 White walls with
        black tiles

9

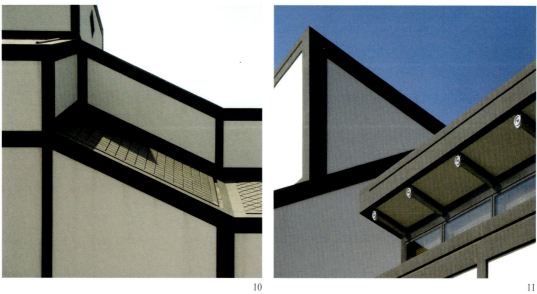

24

10

11

A New Roof for Old

Pei has replaced the traditional wooden structure of Suzhou architecture with steel and glass which allows natural daylight to permeate the building, and has broken with the traditional Suzhou style of large sloped roofs which strictly limited the entrance of natural light. He has created a geometric sloped roof, with a complex of carefully integrated directional lines in harmony with the traditional slopes of the surrounding buildings.

The ingeniously adapted geometric glazed clearstory of the central roof creates a subtle pattern of glass skylights. The application of stone around the roof and the lower white walls below harmonizes the whole style of the building. Pei has used grey black granite as a substitute for the traditional Chinese black tiles which require considerable maintenance. The granite is cut in diamond shapes to add a three dimensional movement to the roof and the changing colours – charcoal grey when dry, black when wet, recreate the traditional Suzhou mixture of structure and movement.

The contrast of glass and granite is both attractive and functional, permitting the sun to shine through the metal louvres with wooden covers into the court and exhibition area. The soft tone of the wood regulates and filters the light creating layers of varying brightness. The windows are no longer the patterned windows of the classical style but an alternating pattern of large clear hexagons and squares, allowing a maximum of daylight thereby eliminating problems inherent in artificial lighting.

12   Chinese black roof tiles   12

13

13,   The glass clearstory
14, 15   Detail of the clearstory

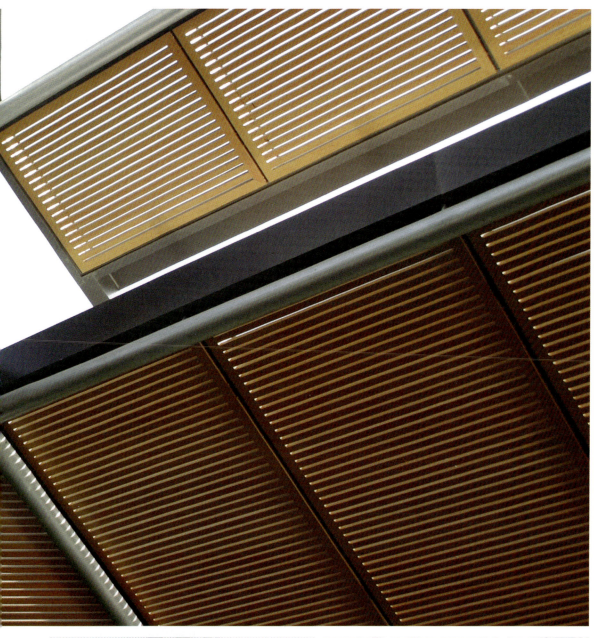

14

15

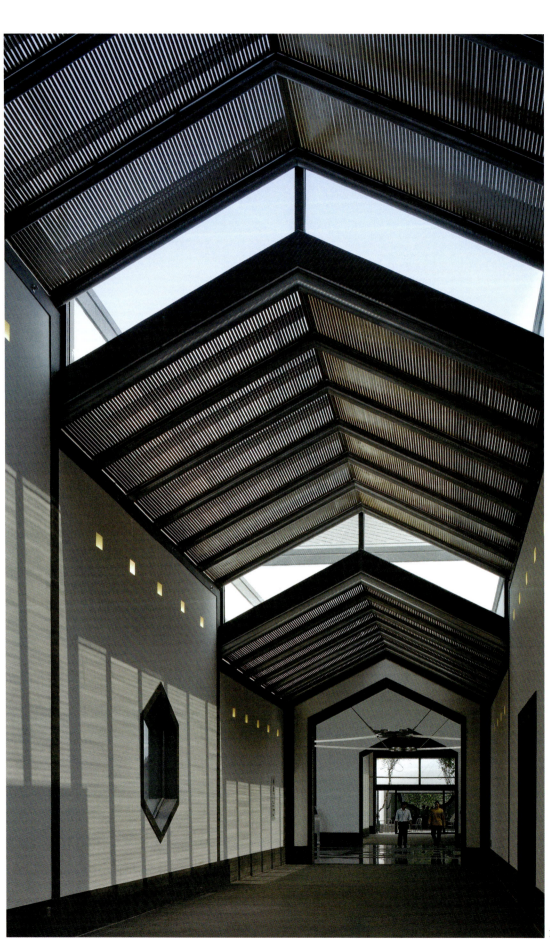

17

18

Sunlight is the designer

Pei has a famous saying: Sunlight is the designer. The combination of sunlight, space and simple geometric lines allows him to play with changing light and shadow, subjecting space to shifts of colour, movement and mood to create a whole range of visual experiences.

19

20

21

The Gateway and the Lobby: Significant Design, Delicate Elegance

The gate at the New Suzhou Museum has a double layer of glass eaves, twin side extensions, and a metal structure. Here Pei's fresh style and modern materials has allowed him to combine the monumental elegance of the noble residences and great courts with the functional requirements of a modern museum. The Lion Forest Garden, the home of his childhood, features the enclosed high wall and a forever closed red gate. The museum gate however required a more open and inviting design, drawing the visitor forwards towards the great lobby situated between the front entrance court and the rear Museum Garden. Both the west and east wings and the front entrance and rear exit around the great lobby give access to all the different areas of the building.

The octagonal design of the lobby utilizes the vertical truss design of classical Suzhou buildings recreated in modern steel. The frame lines of the roof, large and small squares and triangles of glass, alternately reveal the white ceiling, as in a geometric painting, with the azure blue sky and floating white clouds leading the eye through and beyond the glass roof.

22   The lobby   22

Garden Atmosphere

One of Pei's trademarks is an interior court which connects the internal and external space of a building, allowing nature to melt into the building. At the new Suzhou Museum the ingenious layout of the garden also includes several smaller courts. The location of the museum garden posed a severe challenge to Pei, for he was determined not to exclude either the traditional Taihu Lake stone nor the limestone he had used at his Fragrant Hills Hotel near Beijing. His aim was to replicate with original materials, and the skill of local craftsmen, the ancient Chinese landscape paintings in a freshly modern Suzhou style garden. The museum garden is surrounded on the east, south and west sides by buildings, and on the north by the Humble Administrator's Garden.

23 The landscape and water garden

23

The garden covers about one fifth of the area of the museum. The pool has a cobbled bottom, a rockery, a small zigzag bridge, an octagonal pavilion and bamboo groves. The landscape court borders the Humble Administrator's Garden, partitioned off by a north wall with an innovative display of sheet stone and rockery. In deference to the Pian Shan Shi Fan built by Shi Tao, one of the famous 'Yangzhou Eight Eccentric Masters', Pei has here sought, as he has explained to us, to employ the wall as the paper of a painting, and the stone as the images. The focus is on the stone. Such an original piece of landscaping, whereby a clear profile and silhouette effect is created, makes this garden an integral unit of the neighbouring Humble Administrator's Garden. The modern and ancient gardens constitute a whole by an organic connection in the artist's conception. The rockery in the landscape court uses carefully chosen sheets of stone as ornaments. The craftsmen cut the large stone into sheets of differing heights and

Coiling wisteria

The temporary exhibition area lies beyond the east wing. This includes a tea house with a wisteria court. The wisteria plant on the southwest wall was selected by Pei himself from the Guangfu nursery where there are cuttings from a wisteria planted by Wen Zhengming, a famous Ming Dynasty painter. Pei is proud of his carefully sought organic symbol for one of the great emblems of Chinese culture: the growth of the wisteria plant is like the coils of a dragon without horns, its branches and tendrils intertwining like the limbs of the great beast, its flowers shaking like its mane tossed in the wind.

29

28

28, 29   Wisteria
30   The wisteria court

Carefully Chosen Trees

Pei has insisted that the shape of the trees in the courts be graceful and the outline as fluid as the building itself is rigid in order to create a deliberate contrast of flexible and rigid lines. There is a bamboo court, pine trees and almonds. To preserve their height these plants were to be pruned as little as possible before being transplanted. One laurel in the south museum garden is already flourishing, having been the first tree to be transplanted according to Pei's instructions: he wanted the guests at the opening ceremony in autumn to enjoy its fragrance.

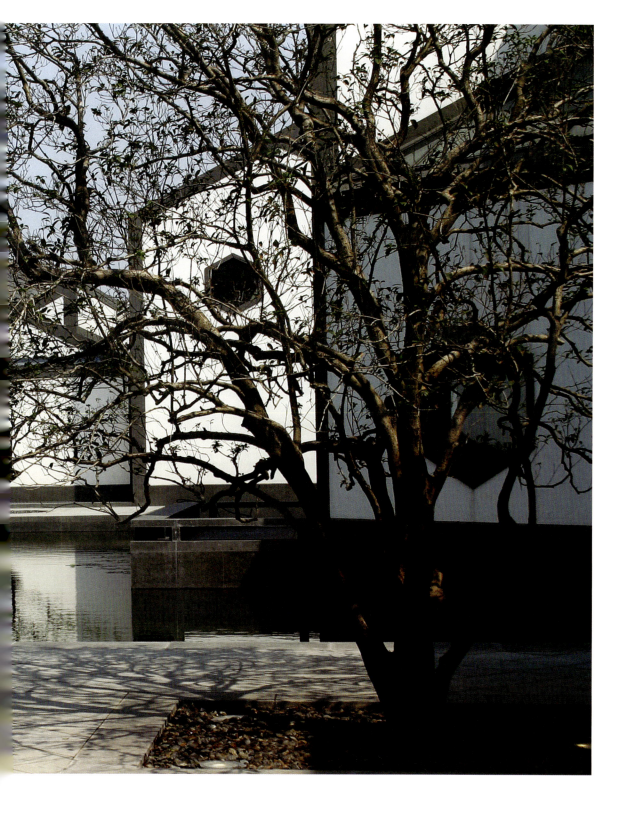

31

32

31 Pine and cypress
32 Feather maple
33 Five-needle pine
34 Bamboo from Anji

33

34

The Street

In order to maintain the integrity of the historic street area where the new Suzhou Museum and Humble Administrator's Garden are located, Pei recommended turning the opposite northeast street into a pedestrian zone. Here the shops use the traditional stele for their shop signs, and the street is decorated with flags bearing folk motifs. On the south side there is a small square near the river where the poplar and willow lazily billow, and the peach blossom blooms resplendently. The ancient style buildings on the two sides of the small square, serve to house various collections of paintings and calligraphy, and provide venues for refreshments.

It was at Pei's suggestion that the road be paved with *jinshan* stone in order to re-create the local character of Suzhou. The technique of processing *jinshan* stone has nearly disappeared, but qualified stone cutters were eventually found and two samples of polished stone were even sent to the USA to be approved personally by Pei.

The northeast street is both elegant and quiet, and provides a dazzling taste of the city, epitomizing the profound change from ancient to modern Suzhou.

35

35, 36, 37 The street

36

37

Zhong Wang Fu (Prince Zhong's Mansion) was built between 1860 and 1863 by Li Xiucheng, known as Prince Zhong by the Taiping rebels, and as Loyal Prince Lee by westerners. It covers a ground area of 10,650 square metres; the building itself is 7,500 square metres. The building complex is grandiose and noble. It is the most perfect building complex of the Kingdom of Heavenly Peace Period (1851-1864), with administrative, residential and garden quarters.

Since the dynasty of the Three Kingdoms, Zhong Wang Fu had been the residence of the nobility. In the Yuan Dynasty, it was modified as Da Hong Temple (Grand Temple). In 1509 in the Ming Dynasty, the censor Wang Xianchen resigned and began his civil life. He built a villa on the relic of Da Hong Temple and called it the Humble Administrator's Garden, which in 1738 was divided in two. The east section was owned Jiang Yongxian, then prefect of Suzhou, who rebuilt it as the Fu Garden; the west section passed to Ye Shikuan who rebuilt it and called it the Book Garden. In June 1860 Li Xiucheng, the military leader of the Taiping rebels occupied Suzhou. He united the garden section of the Humble Administrator's Garden and the residence complex of the east and west sections, thereby creating the Zhong Wang Fu as the Prince's residence. For defence purposes Li Xiucheng added two flanking east and west pavilions at the outer gates of the administration building, and several watch towers.

In 1863 Li Hongzhang occupied Suzhou, and Zhong Wang Fu became the residence of the Jiangsu provincial governor. He ordered the modification of the gate of Zhong Wang Fu according to the provisions of the administration of the Qing Dynasty. The two flanking pavilions and the east and west outer gates of the administration were demolished together with the brilliant paintings on the gateway and beams. Fortunately,

1

the two "Dancing Phoenixes and Peony" paintings on the rear purlin in the second chamber in the main hall survived. In 1866 the office of the provincial governor of Jiangsu moved elsewhere. In 1871 Zhang Wanzhi, a native of Nanpi in Hebei province, senior scholar in the period of the Emperor Guangxu, assumed the Jiangsu governorship, and took up residence in the eastern section of Zhong Wang Fu.

En Xi, deputy principal governor, together with three officials from the Imperial Textile Manufactory of Suzhou ordered the creation of a Guildhall, and in 1872 the middle garden and the east and west section of the residence were joined to make the Zhi (now Hubei) Guildhall, and the attached gardens reverted to being called the Humble Administrator's Garden.

In 1958, the Suzhou Museum began preparations for its official debut to the public at the site of Zhong Wang Fu which took place on New Year's Eve 1960. In 2006 it became part of the new Suzhou Museum.

The Zhong Wang Fu preserves some rare artefacts such as the window lattice with its dragon and phoenix ornaments, the stone lion, some 400 Suzhou style paintings and nine handsome wall paintings. The building also has the largest indoor ancient opera stage in South China .and many noble plant specimens, including a cutting from a wisteria planted by Wen Zhengming.

The collection of Zhang Zhongxian, a native of Suzhou and resident in Hong Kong is exhibited. The western section has been restored to its original appearance as the grand residence of Zhang Luqian, of the Guangxu reign, and the partial garden adjoining the Humble Administrator's Garden. The north section contains the library and the middle section the artefacts from the original Zhong Wang Fu from the Kingdom of Heavenly Peace Period. The restored main hall shows where Li Xiucheng presided at military gatherings.

1   The main hall

3

4

2   The cloister

3   The theatre

4   A screen with a poem

5

6

7

5   The restored chapel
6   The restored regimental hall
7   Four-sided hall

8

9

8   Hall of Woqiu
9   Li Xiucheng

10

11

10, 11   Show of artefacts from the original
         Zhong Wang Fu from the Taiping
         Heavenly Kingdom Period
12   A wisteria planted by Wen
         Zhengming, a famous Ming dynasty
         painter

12

The Suzhou Museum has a collection of about 1,160 pieces dating from the Neolithic period to modern China. The two ground floor western galleries, with an interior shaped like an octagonal pagoda, show the collection of the National Treasures from the Wu Pagoda – from the Hu Qiu Pagoda and the Rui Guang Pagoda. Such treasures are filled with an aura of holiness. The exhibits known as the Wu Relic Treasures at the south side of the ground floor include various styles: Neolithic pottery and jade; Spring and Autumn Period bronze and jade, Six Dynasties Period celadon and Five Dynasty 'secret-colour' porcelain and Zhang and Wang Tomb Relics. The series of Wu Arts display exquisitely carved objects from a Ming scholar's study, porcelain, jade, bamboo, wood and ivory carvings, folk artcrafts, embroidery / tapestry. The exhibition area of Wu Painting and calligraphy on the second floor of the major exhibition area contain choice paintings and calligraphy.

1

2

5

3

4

1   Faint Dawn

        Neolithic pottery and jade

2   Bronze and jade objects of powerful families from the Spring and Autumn Period

3, 4   Celadon and Yue war, Celadon from the Six Dynasties Period

        Secret Colour porcelain from the Five Dynasties Period

5   Luxury objects from city life

        Treasures from the Zhang Tomb, Yuan Dynasty and the Wang Tomb, Ming Dynasty

6

7

6, 7　Hu Qiu Pagoda Treasures
8　　Rui Guang Pagoda Treasures

8

9

10

11

12

9   Ming scholar's study
10   Precious examples of moulding
       porcelain
11, 12   The peak quality of jade carving

13

14

13, 15 Scholar's implements
Tools for painting and calligraphy
14, 16 Objects from a scholar's table
Arts and crafts

15

16

17, 18   Sacred objects
          bamboo, wood and ivory carvings

19   Fortune and luck
          folk arts and crafts

17

18

19

20

20 The life of luxury
embroidery / tapestry
21 Leisure area

21

22

23

24

22, 23, 24   The Painting Hall, Song Pavilion

25 Wu Painting & calligraphy

4

5

3. Rhinoceros horn cup
Ming
Length 68 cm, Diameter of mouth 18.5 – 15 cm
Donated by Wang Jichang.

3

6

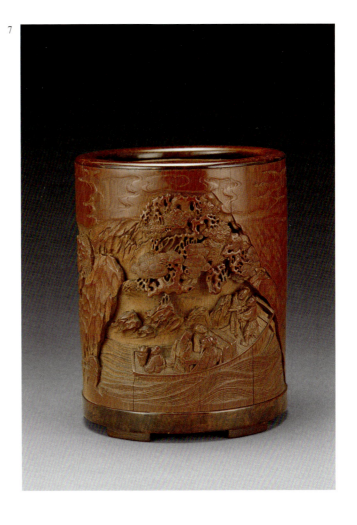

7

4. *Tianhuang* soapstone old man
Qing
Height 5.8 cm

5. Bamboo carved *He He*, two
immortals of harmony and union
Qing
Height 9.8 cm, Width 10.4 cm

6. Censer made of plum tree root
Ming
Length 44.5 cm, Width 9 cm

7. Bamboo brush pot engraved with Su
Dongpo visiting Chibi, the Red Cliff, at
night
Qing
Height 17.4 cm, Diameter of mouth 14 cm

8

9

8. Amber seals
Modern
Length 2.6 cm, Width 2.2 cm, Height 7.1 cm

9. Ink stone from the Chuanshi Lou collection
Qing
Length 9.4 cm, Width 9 cm, Height 0.8 cm

This ink stone is made from She stone from the Kangxi period. Three *zhuan* (seal) style characters *chuan shi lou* are inscribed in intaglio on its base.

Chuanshi Lou was the private library of Xu Qianxue, a *jinshi* (a successful candidate in the imperial examinations) from the Kangxi period. Xu Qianxue (1631-1694), a native of Kunshan, held important positions as Scholar of the Cabinet and Minister of Justice.

10. Ink blocks in the shapes of ten treasures of a scholar's study
Qing
Length of box 26.5 cm, Width 13 cm, Height 3 cm
Donated by He Zeying and He Zehui

These ten ink blocks were made by Wu Tianzhang, also named Zhuo, an eminent ink maker belonging to the Xiuning School of Huizhou during the Kangxi period. The ink blocks are in the shapes of musical instruments, ink stone, paper, brush, paper weight, wrist rest, bamboo pot, sword, precious stone and books. The box is colourfully decorated with gold, silver, blue and green. The decorations on the ink blocks are lightly coloured, exquisite and pleasing to both mind and eye.

10

11. Statue of Immortal Iron-stick Li
carved from *huangyang* wood
Qing
Height 15.5 cm

12. Nut-shaped *zisha* brush washer
Chen Mingyuan
Qing
Height 3.7 cm, Length 9.9 cm, Width 8.3 cm

13. Gilded birdcage made from
zitan wood
Modern
Length 19 cm, Height 21.5 cm, Width 19 cm

11

12

13

14

14. Eleven-faced Guanyin in bronze

Song

Height 23.5 cm

These two statues were excavated from the Yunyan Temple of Huqiu. The eleven-faced Guanyin stands on waisted lotus flower pedestals, with one foot slightly forward, as if walking. Standing Buddhist statues come from the tradition of Sakyamuni preaching while travelling. It is said that after his enlightenment, Sakyamuni travelled around the northwest part of India for forty years to preach. Standing Buddhist statues are also called the statues of travelling preachers.

There are ten faces on top of the head of Guanyin. One face is on the top, four in the middle and five on the bottom. Guanyin wears a heavenly robe, a flowing sash in the right hand which is in the healing mudra. The lower left hand holds a treasure flask. The whole body is adorned with gem stones, ear rings, necklaces, pendants, bracelets and other jewels. A long pearl necklace hangs from neck to feet. There is a small hole on the back to hold up a halo, but the halo was not found.

15

15. Sutra box made of *nanmu* wood

Song

Length 37.8 cm, Width 19.2 cm, Height 21 cm

This box was discovered at the Yunyan Temple of Huqiu in 1957. It is made of *nanmu* wood, painted with lacquer outside. It has exquisitely made gold and silver flakes decorating the edges and joints, with lotus flower and grass patterns on them. The box is fastened by two rows of round nails. There are gold-plated lotus flowers on its four corners. A pair of flying phoenixes decorates the middle of the box. The hinges between the lid and body of the box look like silkworms. Seven volumes of the Lotus Sutra are stored inside.

16. Pearl shrine for Buddhist relics

Song

Height 122.6 cm

This shrine was discovered on the third floor of the Heavenly Palace of Ruiguang Pagoda in 1978. Two lines of Chinese characters in regular script are written in white lacquer on the front of the black outer case: "the pearl shrine for Buddhist relics from the third floor of the Ruiguang pagoda".

The shrine, which is made of *nanmu* wood, consists of a pedestal, a Buddhist palace and a pole. The pedestal is octagonal, standing on short feet. Above the feet is a double-layered square structure with a constricted waist. There are three doors carved on each side of the square structure, above the structure are eight lions cast in silver. The surface then recedes into a flat base. There are two donors in semicircles carved on each side of the receding surface. Above that there is another square structure and a flat base, with eight wooden lions on each side. There are rails on the pedestal, encircling a wavy sea. A gold painted holy mountain rises from the sea and a nine-headed dragon decorated with silver beads flies between the mountain and sea. Eight auspicious clouds made of gold painted wood rise from the sea, with four wood-carved Kings of Heaven and four Ladies of Heaven standing on the clouds to guard the holy pillar. The octagonal pillar is green and gold in colour, with the names of seven Buddhas inscribed with gilded intaglio lines, in regular, cursive, *li* (official style) and *zhuan* (seal style) scripts. A Buddhist prayer in Sanskrit is also inscribed on the pillar.

A gourd shaped greenish ceramic bottle containing the Buddhist relics and two sheets of woodblock printed Buddhist prayers are stored inside the pillar. Above the pillar is a shrine decorated with gold and silver floral spray designs; a gold painted wood Buddha sits inside. Above that is another small lacquer shrine which houses a gold bottle. An octagonal canopy adorned with strings of pearls covers the shrine, its ridges are eight dragons made from gold or silver strings.

There is a pole above the canopy, with a crystal ball on the top, wrapped in silver strings, shining brightly, meaning "to share the light of Buddha around the world".

16

17

17. Gingko wood inner box with colour portraits of the Four Kings of Heaven.

Song

Height 123 cm, Width 42.5 cm

This box was discovered on the third floor of the Heavenly Palace of Ruiguang Pagoda in 1978. It is a two-layered box which houses the pearl shrine for Buddhist relics. It is made of gingko wood, consisting of five square boxes stacked together. There is an inscription on the inside, "recorded on 18th of April, the sixth year of Dazhong Xiangfu reign" of the Song Dynasty. The Four Kings of Heaven are painted in colour on the outside of the box.

Originally the Four Kings of Heaven were characters from Indian legend, later they became guardian warriors of Buddhist text. The composition of the portraits is well proportioned and the expressions of the figures are vivid, heroic, majestic and full of power. Exuberant natural colours were used, making the portraits realistic and full of movement. The style of these portraits is reminiscent of the Tang painter Wu Daozi. The brush stroke and ink wash are forceful and the willow-leaf shaped lines are full of change and movement. The painter was exceptionally skilful and these portraits are almost perfect.

17   Detail

18. Gilded bronze stupa

Five Dynasties

Height 36.8 cm, pedestal 15 x15 cm

This stupa was discovered in the centre of the third floor of the Ruiguang Pagoda in 1978. It is square and can be disassembled into five parts: the pole, the banana-leaf shaped four corners, the main body and a bronze lid and pedestal decorated with sixteen luohans. This stupa is in Indian style, with Buddhist stories carved around the main body and thirty two stories carved on the outside of the banana-leaf shaped corners. There are statues of the Four Kings of Heaven standing inside. The pole is one third of the height of the whole stupa. The pedestal of the pole is shaped like an upside down lotus flower. There are five Buddhist wheels on the pole.

18

19

19. Sutra box with inlaid shells

Song

Length 34.8 cm, Height 12.7 cm, Width 13.7 cm

This box was discovered on the third floor of the Heavenly Palace of the Ruiguang Pagoda in 1978. It is made of wood, painted with black lacquer all over. Inside the Fahua Sutra is written in gold on greenish paper.

The box has three parts: the lid, the body and the pedestal. The lid is rectangular, decorated with three groups of floral patterns on the top, inlaid with a semicircular crystal in the middle and colourful gem stones around. There are pomegranate and peony spray patterns inlaid around the four sides of the box, meaning "many children and grandchildren". The pedestal has sixteen niches decorated with gilded lacquer auspicious grasses, resplendent and magnificent.

20

20. Celadon pot with five spouts

Three Kingdoms

Diameter of belly 22 cm, Height 30 cm

This pot was excavated from the tomb of Sun Jian, father of Sun Quan, the King of Wu, in the southern part of Suzhou City. Pots with five spouts appeared as burial utensils from the mid to the late Eastern Han Dynasty. Buildings, birds and animals, and human figures were added as decorations during the Six Dynasties and Western Jin period. It was also called a 'spirit pot', a 'funeral pot', a 'grain warehouse' and a 'converting pot'. It was used as a burial utensil for the deceased to store grain. Pots with five spouts developed from the Eastern Han period, their designs and decorations became more and more complicated and elaborate. Human figures, birds, animals, buildings and various forms of entertainments were built on top of their main bodies. Some pots also had sculptured stone tablets on tortoise pedestals, with inscriptions in intaglio lines, recording the date, place and auspicious words.

21

21. Olive green celadon lotus flower shaped bowl and saucer from Yue kiln

Five Dynasties

Overall height: 13.5 cm

Bowl: Height 8.9 cm, Diameter of mouth 13.8 cm, Diameter of foot ring 8.1 cm

Saucer: Height 6.6 cm, Diameter of mouth 14.9 cm, Diameter of foot ring 9.3 cm

This celadon lotus flower shaped Yue ware has two parts, a bowl and a saucer. The bowl has an upright mouth, a deep belly and a foot ring. The saucer is shaped like a dou, waisted with an everted mouth and a flared foot ring. The waisted part of the saucer has no decoration, but the bowl and the saucer are decorated with lotus flower patterns in shallow relief. The bowl is shaped like a lotus flower in bloom. The design is very skilful with soft lines, giving a dignified and elegant feel.

It has a green glaze all over, thick but evenly applied, smooth and lustrous like jade. The body is white with a tint of grey and its texture is fine with even and pure grains. The base of the saucer is flat with a hole in the middle. Alongside the hole, there are two characters representing the name of the maker, Xiang Ji. There are densely congregated slanting burn marks on the base, typical of celadon ware from the Five Dynasties period.

'Olive green' wares are celadon produced from Yue kilns along the shores of Shanglin Lake in Zhejiang during the Tang, Five Dynasties and Song periods. Yue ware reached its peak during the Tang and Five Dynasties period. This piece has been authenticated by porcelain experts all over China as one of the rarest celadon wares. Thirteen celadon pieces were excavated in 1987 at Famen Temple. It was recorded on the stele unearthed at the same time that these thirteen pieces were 'olive green' wares from the Yizong reign of the Tang Dynasty. This excavation opened a new chapter in the study of 'olive green' porcelain. An international conference on 'olive green' porcelain was held in Shanghai in 1995 and masterpieces of 'olive green' ware from all parts of China were gathered in Shanghai. Among them, this bowl and saucer unearthed in Huqiu Pagoda was the most excellent. All experts agreed that it represents the best celadon Yue ware, a rare example of 'olive green' porcelain. It is one of the three national treasures of the Suzhou Museum.

22

22. Jun ware drum-shaped brush washer with raised nail-head pattern
Song

Height 9.2 cm, Diameter of mouth 23.9 cm, Diameter of base 17.5 cm

This is a typical brush washer as used by the literati. It was made in the Jun kiln, one of the five most famous kilns of the Song Dynasty. The colour of Jun ware is very unpredictable and uncontrollable by the craftsmen, so was very difficult to copy in later generations. This washer is shaped like a drum, with raised nails and string patterns along the rim and on the belly. It is elegantly made, simple, classical and stylish. The inside glaze has unevenly spread fine lines which are typical in Jun ware and known as 'crawling earthworm lines'. There is a horizontal line carved on the base of the washer, indicating that this washer is among the biggest of its kind.

23

23. Blue and white dish with dragon and sea wave design

Xuande reign period, Ming

Height 4 cm, Diameter of mouth 18.9 cm, Diameter of base 12 cm

The middle of this dish is a double-lined blue ring, decorated with sea waves and a white five footed dragon in *anhua* style. Its outside is decorated with sea waves, rocks and two white five footed dragons.

This dish is a typical example of imperial ware from the Ming Xuande reign.

24. White glazed gourd-shaped oblate flask with two ear handles

Yongle reign, Ming

Height 29.1 cm, Diameter of mouth 3.4 cm,
Diameter of base 6.5 × 5 cm

This flask has a white body, with a translucent glaze all over. The parts with thick glaze have a tint of greyish blue. Overall, the flask has a light greyish blue colour similar to a freshwater prawn. The effect is unique, although this kind of white glazed porcelain was very popular during the Yongle reign.

24

25

26

25. Yellow dish with green dragon design

Zhengde reign, Ming

Height 3.9 cm, Diameter of mouth 18.6 cm, Diameter of base 12.9 cm

This dish has a yellow-glazed background with green-glazed decoration. A similar dish was first fired during the Yongle Reign. The method of glazing was strictly controlled and used only on imperial wares. Only members of the imperial family were allowed to use yellow-glazed wares during the Ming and Qing dynasties. There was also a strict ranking system.

26. Saucers with chrysanthemum spray patterns and diamond shaped rims

Hongwu reign, Ming

Height 2.7 cm, Diameter of mouth 19.5 cm,
Diameter of base 12.7 cm, Diameter of belly ring 5.4 cm

There are ten such saucers in the Suzhou Museum, either in underglazed red or in blue and white. Their main shapes, sizes and decorations are identical. The differences among them are the decorations on their belly rings in the middle, with crab-apple sprays, peony sprays, chrysanthemum sprays, *ruyi* shaped flowers and others. The saucer is a small shallow dish for holding a cup and has become an inseparable part of a tea set since the Song Dynasty.

The bodies of these saucers are white, fine and heavy. The glazing is rich and smooth, white with a tint of green. One saucer has underglazed red as background and white floral sprays as decoration.

27

28

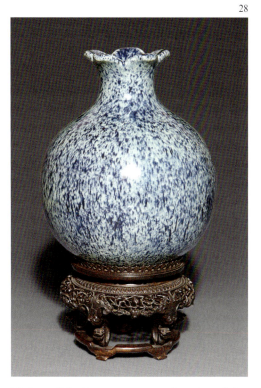

27. Blue and white dish with red-glazed dragon and sea wave design
Qianlong reign, Qing
Height 8.7 cm, Diameter of mouth 47.9 cm,
Diameter of base 28.7 cm

28. Snow-flake blue pomegranate-shaped *zun* (wine vessel) with an inverted mouth
Yongzheng reign, Qing
Height 18.2 cm, Diameter of mouth 7.6 cm,
Diameter of base 6.8 cm, Diameter of belly 15.6 cm

29

29. *Famille rose* bowls and dish with plum and magpie design from the Juren Tang Collection
Republic of China
Diameter of mouth of the dish 15 cm, Diameter of mouths of the bowls 14.5 cm, 12.6 cm, 10.7 cm, 9.2 cm
Donated by Yuan Jingzhen

Juren Tang was the residence of Yuan Shikai at Zhongnanhai in Beijing. It was built by Empress Dowager Cixi, originally named Haiyan Tang. This dinner set was donated to the museum by Yuan Shikai's thirteenth daughter Yuan Jingzhen (Zijing), a genuine and rare example of Hongxian porcelain. It can be used as a yardstick to authenticate Hongxian porcelain.

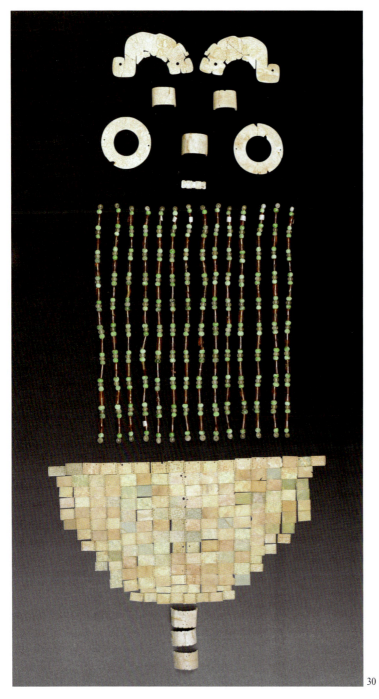

30

30. Jade burial suit
Spring and Autumn Period
circa 150 cm

This burial suit was excavated from the imperial tomb of the Kingdom of Wu, Spring and Autumn period. It consists of a face mask, a beaded top, jade pants and a jade cover for the genitals.

The jade face mask has eight pieces. The tiger-shaped adornments represent eyebrows, slight smaller arched adornments represent eyes, bigger arched adornment represents the nose, jade rings represent the cheeks and the jade mouth piece represents the mouth. The jade mask covers the face of the deceased.

The beaded top is of red agate tubes, green gem stones, cream agate beads and transparent crystal beads stringed together.

The jade pants and the cover for the genitals consist of thirty six pieces.

There are patterns carved on the face mask, pants and genital cover. The carving is fluent and exquisite.

30   Detail

30   Detail

31

31. White jade plaque with human figures and an inscription of *zi* and *gang* characters

Ming

Length 3.5 cm, Width 2.9 cm

This jade plaque is rectangular, with relief carvings on both sides. Its colour is translucent and white. Two characters, *zi* and *gang*, are carved on the back of the plaque in intaglio *zhuan* (seal) script as seals. The maker of the plaque was Lu Zigang, a native of Suzhou, an eminent jade craftsman from the Jiajing and Wanli reigns of the Ming dynasty. He was one of the best jade carvers in China and was renowned for his choice of jade and his carving skills. The plaque uses the best quality jade. Its design is simple and fresh, with vivid human figures, steady and skilful knife work, flowing and sincere calligraphy. It is a rare masterpiece.

32. Jasper octagonal brush washer with two ear handles and lotus design

Qing

Height 8.4 cm, Length 43 cm, Width 29.3 cm

33

33. Three-footed jasper toad
Ming
Length 49 cm, Width 28 cm, Height 13.8 cm

Emperor Xuanling of Zhou was considered to be the founder of the jade carving trade. The former headquarter of jade trade in Suzhou was located in the Temple of Emperor Zhou. This jasper toad was the sacred deity in the temple where members of the jade trade worshipped. It weighs 25.5 kg, exquisitely carved out of a single piece of natural jasper by a master jade craftsman. It is vivid and lifelike. Toads have always been treated as sacred animals by the ancient Chinese although they are not good looking. Three-footed toads are especially auspicious because people believe they can spit out gold and are symbols of good fortune.

34

34. Nephrite elephant
Qing
Height 9.7 cm, Length 14.8 cm,
Width 6.4 cm

This elephant is carved on a piece of nephrite - the most precious jade. The standing elephant is big and plump, looking back from the right, with a boy at his back. The boy holds a tree branch in his left hand and two chrysanthemum flowers in his right. His left leg bends and his right leg straightens, as if he is climbing up the elephant. He looks relaxed and playful, vivid and lifelike.

35

太湖秋霽畫圖開天盡烟帆片片來見說西施歸
去後捧心遲上城王臺西施絕代不堪拍獨倚
危闌吹洞簫七十二峯烟浪裏不知何處是夫樹
夫樹山與洞庭連半沒蒼波羊入烟堪信鷗惠載
西子館娃宮在五湖邊雲擁空山萬木秋故宮何
在水東流高臺不稱西施意鄞向烟波弄釣舟
畫竹遂寫近作
至正甲辰八月五日余適游靈巖歸德機忽持此紙命
四絕於上黃鶴山人王蒙書

35. Bamboo and rock

Wang Meng

Yuan

Hanging scroll, water and ink on paper; Length 77.2 cm,
Width 27 cm

Donated by Gu Gongshuo

Wang Meng(? – 1385), style name Shuming and
literary name Huanghe Shanqiao, was a native
of Huzhou. He was accomplished in landscape
painting and is known as one of the 'Four
Masters of the Yuan period'.

The top half of the painting has a few
branches of bamboo in black ink, the bottom
half has rocks of different sizes which are
outlined with fine brush strokes and shaded
with light ink wash. There are four four-line
poems written in the middle of the painting.
The calligraphy is exquisite and the poem is
outstanding. Wang Meng is renowned for his
landscape paintings but it is very rare to see
his bamboo and rock. This painting combines
poetry, calligraphy and painting in one and is
extremely precious.

Wang Meng painted this hanging scroll
for Zhang Deji at the 24th year of the Zhizheng
reign (1364) when he was fifty seven. It has
been recorded in "Jingxu Zhai's Recollections
of Paintings" and "The Guoyun Lou Book of
Calligraphy and Painting".

36

37

36. Deep river in May

Wen Zhengming

Ming

Hanging scroll, ink and water on paper, Length 127.5 cm, Width 31 cm

Donated by Gu Gongshuo

Wen Zhengming (1470 – 1559), original name Wen Bi, first style name Zhengming then changed to Zhengzhong, literary name Hengshan Jushi, was a native of Suzhou. He learnt literature from Wu Kuan, calligraphy from Li Yingzhen and painting from Shen Zhou. He was accomplished in calligraphy, but excelled in painting. He shares the same reputation as Shen Zhou and is revered as the grandmaster of the Wu School. He is also one of the so-called 'Four Masters of the Ming'.

The composition of this painting has great depth, with towering and imposing mountain peaks. The brushwork is fresh and solid, fine lines and light ink wash depicts exuberant and verdant vegetation. The technique of this landscape came from Wang Meng of the Yuan Dynasty, but the style and spirit belongs to Wen himself. It is a masterpiece of fine brushwork. It was painted in the *Bingshen* year of the Jiajing reign (1539) when Wen Zhengming was sixty seven.

37

37. Boat returning home

Dai Jin

Ming

Handscroll, ink and colour on silk, Length 36.5 cm, Width 76.5 cm

Donated by Gu Gongshuo

Dai Jin (1388 – 1462), style name Wenjin, literary names Jingan and Yuquan Shanren, was a native of Hangzhou. He was accomplished in landscape, figurative, bird and flower paintings. He is revered as the grandmaster of the Zhe School.

The beginning of the scroll shows three characters "boat returning home" written in *li* (official) style by Tu Fei. It also contains colophons and postscripts by sixteen high-ranking officials from that period, fifteen of whom were natives of Suzhou. The postscripts reveal that this painting was a farewell gift to Zhang Mengduan and it was painted in July at the 6th year of the Zhengtong reign (1441).

38

38. Flowers and birds

Shen Zhou

Ming

Album, ink and water on paper, Length 30.3 cm, Width 52.4 cm

Donated by He Zeying and He Zehui

Shen Zhou (1427 – 1509), style name Qinan, literary name Baishi Weng, also known as Master Shitian, was a native of Suzhou. He had never been successful in his official career. He was a poet and a writer. His calligraphy was greatly influenced by Huang Shangu and his painting was exceptional. He developed his own style by learning from various schools from the Yuan and Song dynasties.

This album has ten paintings. Wen Zhenming wrote four characters *shi weng mo miao* (excellent works by Master Shi) in *li* (official) style at the beginning of the album. One painting depicts a duckling and the other nine paintings depict nine kinds of flowers, red apricot, lily magnolia, peony, holly, lily, begonia, tricolour amaranth, lotus and pomegranate. This album used the 'boneless' technique and Shen Zhou painted it after he reached the age of sixty one.

38

41

39

40

39. Black bamboo
Xia Chang
Ming
Hanging scroll, ink and colour on paper, Length 48.3 cm,
Width 25.8 cm

40. Peach blossom garden
Zhou Chen
Ming
Hanging scroll, ink and water on silk, Length 161.2 cm, Width 102.3 cm
Donated by Zhou Shoujuan

41. Landscapes
Gong Xian
Qing
Hand scroll, ink and water on paper,
Length 35 cm, Width 283.3 cm
Gong Xian (1618 – 1689),
another name Qixian, style
name Banqian, literary names
Banmu and Haochai Zhangren.
He was a native of Kunshan
but lived mostly in Jinling. He
was accomplished in poetry
and writing and excelled in
landscape painting. He is one
of the so-called 'Eight Masters
of Jinling'. His writings include
"On painting" and "Collections
from the Hall of Fragrant
Grass".

42

42. Farming village

Tang Yin

Ming

Hanging scroll, ink and colour on silk, Length 113.4 cm, Width 61 cm

Tang Yin (1470—1523), style names Bohu and Ziwei, literary names Liuru Jushi, Taohua Anzhu and Taochan Xianli, was a native of Suzhou. He had made the first place in the imperial exam in Yingtian Fu (Nanjing) at the 11th year of the Hongzhi reign (1498), but was found to have cheated in the exam and was dismissed from office the following year. He named himself 'the first romantic scholar of southern China' after he had returned to his hometown. He was accomplished as a poet and a writer. He studied painting with Zhou Chen and excelled his teacher.

He also studied with Shen Zhou and was greatly influenced by Li Cheng, Li Tang, Zhao Mengfu and Wang Meng. He also had his own distinctive style and enjoyed great fame among the 'Four Masters of the Ming'.

This is the masterpiece painted by Tang during his middle age. It combines both southern and northern styles, fresh and full of free spirit. It has a poem written on the painting, commenting on the society and politics.

43. Calligraphy on a fan

Weng Tonghe

Qing

Paper, Length 31.5 cm, Width 60.5 cm

Weng Tonghe (1830 – 1904) was a native of Changshu County of Suzhou. His style name was Shengfu, literary names Shuping, Pingsheng, Songchan and Wubu Jushi. He came first in the imperial exam in the 6th year of the Xianfeng reign (1856). He was the teacher of both Emperor Tongzhi and Emperor Guangxu. He was one of the most important officials who supported 'the reform of Wuxu'. After the failure of the reform, he was dismissed from office and returned to his hometown. He was renowned for his powerful calligraphy.

Donated by Wu Hufan.

43

44

44. Gathering of literati in the western garden

Li Shida

Ming

Donated by Gu Gongshuo

Hand scroll, ink and colour on paper, Length 25.8 cm, Width 140.5 cm
Li Shida, literary name Yanghuai, was a native of Suzhou. He was a *jinshi*
(a successful candidate in the imperial examinations) of the 2nd year of the
Wanli reign (1574), accomplished in figurative and landscape paintings.
He lived into his eighties.

45. Calligraphy on a fan

Peng Dingqiu

Paper, Length 31.5 cm, Width 60.5 cm

Donated by Wu Hufan

45

46

46. Silk embroidery of a portrait of Ji Gong

Shen Shou
Qing
Length 88 cm, Width 34 cm

This portrait of Ji Gong is embroidered on a piece of light blue silk. Ji Gong holds a banana leaf fan, walking towards two jars of wine in front of him. His eyes are glued to the wine, with a big smile and vivid expression on his face. The artist used a western technique to portray the colour and shadows of Ji Gong's face, neck, clothes and the wine jars. The shadows reflect the light source, reminiscent of western style sketches. Its colour and stitches thoroughly reflect Ji Gong's love of wine and his slight drunkenness. The cords on the jars are also perfectly depicted, giving a very realistic feel.

Shen Shou was a famous embroiderer of the Su School of the Qing period. She invented true to life embroidery techniques and her works were extremely realistic. This embroidery was made in the 31st year of the Guangxu reign (1905) and Shen Shou was 31 years old.

47

48

47. Silk tapestry with phoenix and peony design
Song
Length 66.8 cm, Width 36.7 cm
Donated by Qian Yong and Xu Yue

48. Silk embroidery of Xinghua Village
The Luxiang Yuan Embroidery House
Ming
Length 85.2 cm, Width 41.8 cm

49. Embroidered two-piece lady's dress with phoenix design
Republic of China
Length of jacket 49 cm, Length of sleeves 41.5 cm, Chest size 38 cm,
Height of collar: 7 cm, Length of skirt 90 cm, Waist size 58 cm

This lady's dress was donated by Yuan Jingzhen, the 13th daughter of Yuan Shikai. It was her wedding dress.

49

Tourist information

Opening hours 9:00-17:00 (Tickets sold until 16:00)
204 Dong Bei Jie
Suzhou Jiangsu China 215001
www.szmuseum.com
Email: admin@szmuseum.com
Tel: +86 (512) 67575666   +86 (512) 67575111
Fax: +86 (512) 67544232
Bus routes 1, 2, 5, 40, 55, 178, 202, 309, 313, 518, 529, 811 and 923 provide
direct transportation to the Museum.
Public Services: Information Desk, Free Brochure and Map, Cloak Room,
Paid Docent Service, Volunteer Guide, Orientation Hall, Umbrella and
Wheel Chair Rental, Audio Tour, Tea House, Gift Shop.